Hyok Kang was born in 1986 in Onsung-kun, the North Hamkyung province of North Korea. *This Is Paradise!* was first published in France following the collaboration with French journalist Philippe Grangereau, who met him at a human rights forum in Prague. Hyok Kang now lives in South Korea.

This Is Paradise! was first published in France
under the title:
Ici, C'est Le Paradis!: Une enfance en Corée du Nord

Also by Philippe Grangereau
Au pays du grand mensonge: Voyage en Corée du Nord

This Is Paradise!

My North Korean Childhood

HYOK KANG

with PHILIPPE GRANGEREAU

translated by SHAUN WHITESIDE

ABACUS

First published in Great Britain in 2005 by Little, Brown
This paperback edition published in 2007 by Abacus
Reprinted 2007, 2009

A CIP catalogue record for this book
is available from the British Library.

ISBN 978-0-349-11865-9

Typeset in Bembo by M Rules
Printed and bound in Great Britain by Clays Ltd, St Ives plc

Papers used by Abacus are natural, renewable and recyclable
products sourced from well-managed forests and certified
in accordance with the rules of the Forest Stewardship Council.

Mixed Sources
Product group from well-managed
forests and other controlled sources
www.fsc.org Cert no. SGS-COC-004081
© 1996 Forest Stewardship Council
FSC

Abacus
An imprint of
Little, Brown Book Group
100 Victoria Embankment
London EC4Y 0DY

An Hachette UK Company
www.hachette.co.uk

www.littlebrown.co.uk

Someone that you have deprived of everything is no longer in your power. He is once again entirely free.

Alexander Solzhenitsyn, *The First Circle*

Contents

Preface

I first met Hyok in Prague, in the spring of 2003. This shy, intelligent boy had been invited to the Czech Republic by a human rights organisation to give an account of his life in North Korea.* Two other refugees, in their forties, had been invited as well. They talked at length about their painful experiences in a North Korean gulag. Young Hyok, probably because of his shyness, didn't dare take the microphone. But the essence of what he had been through was displayed on the picture rails of the hall hired for the occasion, in the form of drawings, some precise, some clumsy, but always imbued with that spontaneous sincerity that you often come across in children. What he had trouble putting into words, he drew marvellously well, with an excellent memory for detail.

---

*Hyok was invited by the People in Need Foundation (PINF), which was holding the fourth conference of the South Korean NGO 'North Korean Human Rights' (NKHR).

This Is Paradise!

After escaping from North Korea in 1998, Hyok had spent four years in China, and so he was able to express himself a little in Chinese, a language I spoke myself. Emboldened by this bridge between us, I invited him out to a Prague restaurant. The young man told me how he had survived famine in North Korea: tree-bark soups, rat hunts with his friends, hours spent digging coal in the galleries of the mine, night-time raids on state farms; the weakening, then death of several of his schoolfriends . . . Hyok related these episodes casually, as though he were talking to me about just another ordinary day. What he had seen with his child's eyes some years previously, millions of other North Koreans had also experienced every day of their lives – and continue to do so today. Because even now, in 2007, famine still rages in North Korea, and kills just as surely as it ever did. 'My dream now,' Hyok joked after all that (as he devoured a large ice-cream smothered in whipped cream), 'is to get fat!'

Hyok is scrawny and short. Like almost all North Korean children, his growth has been stunted by chronic malnutrition. Delving into his memory, Hyok was still able to evoke startling moments from his everyday life in North Korea: the incredible teachings inculcated in him at school, the level of complete indoctrination to which the entire population was subjected in this Stalinist paradise, immersed in the veneration of the 'Great Leader'.

Preface

Later, Hyok told me of his flight to China, how he had crossed the border, the Tumen river, which is frozen in winter; the four years he spent struggling in Manchuria, where the Chinese police ruthlessly hunt down illegal North Korean immigrants; and finally his long and dangerous escape to South Korea in 2002 – via Vietnam, Laos, Cambodia and Thailand.

Three months after my Prague conversation with Hyok, I went to meet him in South Korea, and it was in Seoul, after a fortnight of collaboration and conversations, that this book began to take shape. I should like to thank Cory Shim, our gifted interpreter, who helped us with this project, as well as Hyok's parents, who enabled me to clarify numerous points.

'When I tell children of my own age in South Korea what life is like in North Korea, most of the time they don't believe me,' Hyok admitted to me one day. What's surprising about that? How can you describe such an improbable country? North Korea is home to one of the most loathsome totalitarian regimes on the planet. It is characterised by an extravagant personality cult, a devastated economy, an empire of lies and propaganda and a gulag holding at least ten thousand prisoners. This *Jurassic Park* of communism distils a mood of Cold War paranoia in which the denunciation of any kind of dissidence is exalted as a virtue. The population is divided into several dozen social 'categories', organised into a hierarchy by the bureaucracy according to their real or supposed loyalty to the 'Dear Leader' Kim Jong-Il (son of the late 'Great Leader' Kim Il-Sung, who died in 1994). The famine that has been wreaking such havoc there since 1993–4 has caused between two and three million deaths among people in the most vulnerable categories, despite massive international aid, most of which was embezzled by the regime to fund its military apparatus. The government in Pyongyang, the capital of North Korea, explains away its food shortages with reference to 'natural disasters', while in fact the causes of the terrible hunger lie in the cruel absurdities and monstrous abuses of power practised by the country's dictatorship.

North Korea is also the most closed state in the world. All kinds of receivers, whether radio or television, are fixed to the official frequencies, and no foreign newspapers are available. However, the number of refugees who have managed to escape this closed country of twenty-three million inhabitants is constantly growing. Some three hundred thousand North Koreans have managed to take refuge in China since the mid-nineties. Of them, several thousand have reached South Korea, at risk to their lives. Nonetheless, and I think it's a shame, few publishers or journalists are interested in their shattering stories.* Here is one of those exceptional testimonies, the testimony of a child, and in that it is unique.

Philippe Grangereau

---

* Only one has so far been published: *Aquariums of Pyongyang: Ten Years in the North Korean Gulag*, by Kang Chol-Hwan and Pierre Rigoulot, Basic Books, 2001.

1

Onsong

The cult of the Great Leader

My name is Hyok. I was born on 20 April 1986 in a village not far from Onsong, a city of three hundred thousand inhabitants in the north-east of the People's Democratic Republic of Korea, very close to both the Chinese border and to Siberia, in Russia. In winter, the temperature drops to below thirty-five degrees. The city is divided into *ku* (districts) and *ban* (classifications) of twenty families. My parents lived in *ban* number three, in a semi-rural zone. The house was like dozens of others built on the same model and lined up in rows. There was a door, a single window, and a roof of curved orange tiles. The walls were white, but they had been painted blue to a height that I must have passed at around the age of eight or nine. Each

1

time the officials of our district came to check the hygiene of the houses, as they regularly did, they ordered us to change the colour of this lower part. The colours changed, green, now blue, now light brown, but all the houses in our *ban* had to be the same colour; perhaps because dwellings, like everything else that exists in North Korea, are the property of the 'people'. That means that nothing really belongs to anyone, because there is no such thing as private property. Since society is more important than the individual, individualism is severely criticised. That is probably the reason for the uniformity imposed on the colour of the houses and, of course, on many other things too.

Inside, our home consisted of two rooms separated by a sliding door. You reached it through the kitchen, where you left your shoes by a coal fire made of brick. This fire extended underneath the floor of the two rooms. This form of brick underfloor heating is called an *ondol*, and is very practical in the winter when the temperature plummets. The floors of the rooms were covered with pale brown varnished floor-paper, and on the walls in the main room hung portraits of Kim Il-Sung and Kim Jong-Il. That was compulsory. You had to call the father: 'Dear respected comrade head of state Great Leader Kim Il-Sung', or more simply 'Comrade Great Leader'. We children had to call him 'Great Leader Grandfather Kim Il-Sung'. For his son, the formula was 'Dear Leader Kim Jong-Il', until Kim Il-Sung's death in 1994; then we had to call him 'Great Leader Kim Jong-Il'. The house's only window lit the end room, which was furnished with a wardrobe stacked with cotton duvets. The dresser for the kitchen utensils was in the first room, by the kitchen.

Our district stood at the foot of some mountains, which were riddled with coal mines. Around here everyone lived off the mines. The good side of this was that you didn't die of cold in winter, as you might have done elsewhere, because our fuel supplies were always guaranteed. In our house, as in all the others, there was a loudspeaker that delivered the broadcasts from Pyongyang. They told you the news, always devoted to the Dear Leader Kim Jong-Il, alternated with songs composed in his honour or to the glory of his father. Some of these devices deteriorated over time and stopped making any sound. But that wasn't the case in our house, where everything was kept in good condition. We also had a radio that received these broadcasts, which was fixed by the authorities to that single station. When a radio imported from abroad didn't come up to the required norms, it had to be taken to a special security office where they switched it to the official station so that we wouldn't hear any other programmes.

There were two big cinemas in Onsong. When a new film came out, as they did every six or seven months, the whole city flocked to see them. An unbelievable crowd . . .

People fought to sit down on the wooden seats. On the programme: battles, fights, expeditions, assaults, attacks, bombing, offensives, ambushes . . . Apart from the war films made by Kim Jong-Il – because our Great Leader adores the cinema – Chinese war films were often shown. Russian war films, although they had been highly prized for a time, had disappeared long since. In 1998, when we fled the country, the cinemas were also showing war films set in the Middle Ages, a glorious era in Korea's history, when it had triumphantly confronted Japan and China. Some films were devoted to the celebrated ruse of the Korean general Yee, who had defeated the Nippons by using armoured ships, the first in the history of the world. Sometimes they inflicted on us yet another episode of the series *The Fate of the People*, telling the story of the Korean War against the 'Southern puppets' and the 'long-nosed imperialists'.

A very wide street ran through Onsong, the only tarmacked street in the whole city. It was lined with residential buildings four or five storeys high and government offices. Right next to this large avenue stood the station, with portraits of Kim Il-Sung and Kim Jong-Il hanging from its façade. It had no name, as with the other streets in the city, because giving names to geographical places could have informed potential enemy invaders, 'long-nosed American imperialists' or 'South Korean puppets'. The tarmacked arterial road led to the foot of a mountain where a communication tower was built, its top lit by a red light. However, in around 1995–6, because of the electricity shortage, the light had gradually begun to fade, turning first orange, then dark brown, before finally going out completely.

In the centre of the city, in Kim Il-Sung Park, there was a huge painting representing the Great Leader. Placed behind glass, it was inlaid into a marble stele more than five metres tall. It showed Kim Il-Sung greeting a crowd and waving a bouquet of flowers. I don't know who painted portraits of that kind, which are very widespread in North Korea, because I have never seen an artist at work. These solemn images were always kept in very good condition. No one dared to amuse themselves by damaging them in any way; such an insult to the Great Leader would have been punished by immediate death. Everyone knew that from primary school onwards.

In Onsong, as elsewhere, there were portraits of Kim Il-Sung all over the place, even in factory courtyards and the galleries of the coal mines. But the one in Kim Il-Sung Park was the biggest. The most impressive monument, however, was a massive bronze statue representing Kim Il-Sung in military uniform surrounded by soldiers. To get to it, you had to climb a mountain by a marble staircase as wide as a boulevard. The ascent took at least twenty minutes. The sculpture was so tall that a schoolboy, no matter how agile, would have had trouble climbing on to the Great Leader's giant shoe. The plinth alone was taller than a grown-up, forcing the visitor to raise his head to look into the statue's eyes. I imagine that this must have been the intention. The bronze Kim Il-Sung, approximately as high as a four-storey building, was dressed in a large coat. Bareheaded, he waved with one hand, while with the other he carried a child on his hip. Behind him stood soldiers with red-starred caps, brandishing machine-guns and rifles: a common theme in North Korea.

The spotlights that illuminated the statue were immense: at least one metre in diameter. I remember that even when the electricity ran out completely, and we didn't have a single bulb to light the city, those spotlights went on shining regardless. In front of the plinth of the statue there were pots of flowers, always carefully watered and replaced the moment they started to fade.

At the back of the esplanade there were two large permanent panels depicting, in high relief, soldiers confronting the Japanese invader.* The monument commemorated the battle of the mountain of Wangche. I wasn't a very good pupil in North Korea, but from my youngest days I knew all about that battle: the troops of Kim Il-Sung had held a position at the top of those very steep heights, and had

---

* Japan occupied Korea between 1910 and 1945.

managed to repel the Japanese soldiers as they tried to climb to the top. The large panel was decorated with a long poem written by Kim Il-Sung himself, telling of his courage in battle.

When I was very small, Kim Il-Sung came to Onsong in person. My father told me that the whole city was cleaned from top to bottom in anticipation of the event. A massive parade had welcomed the Great Leader, with all the inhabitants mobilised to sing in chorus, salute in unison and wave bouquets of flowers as he passed. Subsequently, a hymn was composed to commemorate his visit. The guest house where he had stayed near Onsong became a sort of little sanctuary with a plaque: no one could use the bed he had slept in, or even enter the room. In fact, all the bedrooms throughout the country where the 'perfect brain' had slept on his many travels have become prohibited places. No one else can sleep there – how could you occupy the same room as 'the sun', the name by which Kim Il-Sung is referred to in North Korea? Consequently, thousands of houses across the country have become little chapels devoted to the cult, or else have simply been locked up for ever.

Parades are a feature of daily life in North Korea. They are part of a very hierarchical ritual. There are three kinds. Parade type one, the most ostentatious, is for when the

Great Leader is being welcomed, and type two, less solemn, is reserved for high-level Party officials. Army generals settle for type three. In the parades of the first type, the people whose responsibility it is to wave the bouquets of flowers and cheer from the front rows are chosen from families of high-ranking Party cadres who are particularly loyal to the Great Leader. Ordinary people are admitted to the front rows only during type-three parades. My father told me he saw a type-two parade, in Namyang, near Onsong, in the late eighties. It was held in honour of the Secretary General of the Chinese Communist Party, Hu Yaobang, who was returning to China at the end of a visit to Pyongyang. All participants had to be checked with metal detectors, even the musicians in the orchestra.

I myself never took part in a welcome ceremony for such an important figure. But even so, and this was true of all children, we had to train collectively during our gymnastics classes at school, as well as almost every weekend, to perform those orchestrated processions. We learned how to salute, how to wave bouquets of flowers, neither too high nor too low, how to march in step . . . all in time with the music. We also had to memorise a certain number of collective dance moves, while holding giant panels inscribed with characters which, placed end to end and seen from a certain distance away, bore slogans such as

'Long live the Workers' Party',* or 'Long live the Great Leader Kim Jong-Il'. We spent hours and hours perfecting our gymnastic moves. The big rehearsals took place on holidays, on the birthdays of Kim Il-Sung and Kim Jong-Il. Then parade competitions were organised between the different schools, and the best one was awarded a diploma.

The power station always switched off electricity at night, plunging the city into darkness. As far as I can remember, when I was small electricity cuts during the day lasted several minutes. Then they gradually became more frequent, and, in around 1995, they started lasting all day, then weeks. This meant that water wasn't being pumped, so we had to turn on the taps and hoard supplies as soon as the electricity came back on. But when the intervals were too long, we had to go and collect water from a village not far from the city. As the only son of the family, I was usually the one chosen for this task, although my father also went from time to time. Even when everyone's resources were exhausted, the statue of Kim Il-Sung continued to light up the night, even more brightly than before in some people's opinion. But no one ever kicked up a fuss on the subject.

---

*Meaning the Communist Party, whose ideology derives both from Stalinism and from '*juché*', a doctrine invented by Kim Il-Sung and based on the idea of self-sufficiency.

Nor about the food that was no longer being distributed by the State, and on which we depended entirely because, apart from the tiny vegetable gardens belonging to the luckiest people, everything was collectively owned. Neither did anyone complain about the hospital. Medication and injections had been free, but that changed and then everything had to be paid for somehow. To have an operation you had to give a bottle of *soju* (rice spirits) to the surgeon.

Executions

In Onsong, it was said that an ox or a cow was much more valuable than a human being, because the animal has ten times as much energy as a man. Cows are very precious tools, and very rare in North Korea. So much so that none could ever be found on sale. Oxen were priceless. When I was still at primary school, I wondered how much you would have to pay for a cow if you killed one by accident. Would you face a firing squad? At any rate, if you stole one you would certainly be executed. But who would dare do that?

Oxen harnessed to a wooden cart with iron-rimmed wheels sometimes acted as a means of transport. Motorised vehicles were rare. In the whole city there were only five tractors, used at the mine, and two military jeeps that ferried the Party cadres around. The tractors were immobilised most of the time by lack of petrol, while the jeeps were propelled by a gas generator fuelled by coal. Every now and then we would see a Mercedes or two; they belonged to the high-ranking Party officials or the army who lived in Pyongyang, the capital, where the privileged had their homes.

The most affluent travelled by bicycle in Onsong, but most people went on foot. In North Korea, people often walk for forty kilometres without grumbling. And they had many reasons for travelling, chief among them being the black market. You bought merchandise that was cheaper in one place to sell it at a higher price somewhere else. And they carried everything on their backs, because even where there were vehicles there was no petrol. Even the trains barely ran anymore. You had to wait two weeks for the Onsong-Pyongyang train, and then another three days before there was a connection. Not even five kilometres an hour! And also, many of the people involved in the black market didn't take the railway, because then they would have been liable to being checked. They walked along the railway tracks where there was less chance of meeting the pale green uniforms of the policemen than on the roads, because many of them weren't carrying the travel permit that you need in North Korea to leave the district where you live. It's very hard to get hold of, unless you grease the palm of the official in the permit office.

Nonetheless, everyone – from beggars to Party cadres – tries to do a bit of smuggling. But woe betide anyone who gets caught!

At the age of nine I saw my first execution, in the grounds of the brick factory. The man had been condemned to death for stealing copper wire from electric pylons to sell in China, crossing the border under the cover of darkness. He was dragged to a recess dug at the foot of the mountain, near a railway track. A train that happened to pass just at that moment, by a barely believable coincidence, stopped to let the passengers watch the scene. Executions were a frequent occurrence in our small city. Five or six a year. But the inhabitants never tired of them. As soon as an execution was announced, they hurried to the place where it was to be performed. The locations often changed, but I don't know why. The children went and stood in the first row, ready to leap forward to pick up the rifle cartridges or the bullets that were left stuck in the execution post after passing through the victim's body. People flocked in huge numbers. Primary and secondary school pupils even skipped school to join the audience, which always consisted of hundreds, even thousands, of people.

Small posters went up in the city several days before each event. When the time came, the condemned man was displayed in the streets before being led to the place of execution, where he was made to sit on the ground, head bowed, so that everyone could get a good look at him. Then the crowd stood aside during the preparations. As in the theatre, a flag was stretched out, behind which the soldiers planted the post and got the condemned man ready. They dressed him in a garment specially designed by army scientists for public executions. It's a greyish one-piece suit made of very thick, fleece-lined cotton, not combed but simply carded, like the insides of the quilts at my grandmother's house. That way, when the bullets are fired, the blood doesn't spurt out all over the place, but is absorbed by this special fabric, which turns red.

Once the flag is removed, the execution can begin. It's conceived as a performance in three acts. The prisoner is attached to a wooden post by two ropes at his chest and his legs. A soldier orders the platoon of three soldiers, 'Attention, take aim, fire!' An initial salvo, aimed at the chest, breaks the first rope, causing the body to sag forward. A second salvo of three bullets hits the top of the man's head, which literally explodes. The brain spills into a big bag supplied for the purpose and placed at the prisoner's feet. In the winter, at temperatures of minus twenty or minus thirty, there's a lot of steam when that happens, because of the difference in temperature between the body and the atmosphere . . . Finally, three bullets are fired at the height of the rope holding the legs. Then the body falls forward, with the torso falling into the bag, and it only remains for the soldiers to give it a few kicks and pull up the sides of the bag to get the corpse inside. My friends loved these performances. They used to say, 'The condemned man bowed to us before he died.' Once it was laced into its bag, the body was thrown on to the back of a truck or a cart. Then it was abandoned somewhere in the mountains without being buried, for the dogs to eat.

My father saw many hangings, a punishment that is reserved for the most serious criminals, for example those known as 'nihilists'.* Hanging is more spectacular, because the condemned man is simply hoisted by a rope to gallows, like a puppet, and his death-throes last several minutes.

Restrictions

The most senior official in Onsong is the city Party Secretary. After that comes the President of the Municipal Administrative Committee, then the people in charge of propaganda and the officials in charge of rationing. Every two weeks, the national system of food distribution allowed

---

* In the true meaning of the word, a nihilist is someone who refuses all forms of social constraint and calls for total freedom. In North Korea, the term refers to the worst enemies of the State.

us a food ration made up of seven parts crushed maize, or sometimes potatoes, to three parts rice. The ration, measured by weight, was, unofficially, calculated according to the category to which the recipient belonged: manual worker, intellectual worker, child, baby, working woman, housewife . . . The last category, for example, received three hundred grams per day of this food cocktail, while a worker received twice as much. Free days (Sundays) were subtracted from the total, however, so that every two weeks each person received twelve rations.

There were often delays in supply. We were used to this. They had begun as early as 1985. However, these gaps in rationing were more or less made up for in the autumn when we were given about an extra hundred kilos of maize. But shortly before the death of Kim Il-Sung, in 1994, the system began to break down. First of all we started receiving only a week of rations every two months. Then the big warehouses of the national reserves, which are guarded by the army, were found to be empty. It was at this point that quantities began to shrink: three days of rations every two months, then forty-eight hours of rations for sixty days . . .

Finally, in 1997 everything came to a sudden halt. That year was the most terrible of all. Officials said that war was around the corner, because the American imperialists and the traitors to our country were preparing to overthrow our national government. That got us moving! The whole city was mobilised. But I will tell you about that later.

Social categories

There were restaurants in Onsong, but shortages had forced them to shut up shop in 1995. Even the restaurant in the Kim Il-Sung Museum, on Wangjiasan mountain, closed around that time. Occasionally some of these State establishments reopened, but only for the banquets of Party officials. The officials were the only people who deserved to be called *tonji* (comrades), apart from soldiers who also called each other 'comrade'. The banquets of the comrade cadres of Onsong were held on the quiet, usually in the evening, and guests entered discreetly by the back door. Otherwise, such a bold gesture in the middle of a famine would have been terribly shocking to everybody. The cadres' meals were always of high quality, and they never went short of meat.

When deliveries of food aid arrived from the United Nations, the cadres in charge of supplying them skimmed off almost everything. There again, they helped themselves on the sly, emptying the warehouses in the middle of the night with their wheelbarrows, which they pushed as quietly as they possibly could. Ordinary people never caught a glimpse of this international food aid. Gradually, everyone started calling the cadres 'dirty dogs'. But being well fed wasn't enough for them: they demanded that the starving workers work even harder. They fixed higher production quotas and extended the compulsory 'criticism and self-criticism meetings' to which they called the hungry population.

These meetings take place at the end of the working day. They involve running through the work that has been done, suggesting improvements, criticising skivers or anyone who has skipped the morning meeting for the reading of texts by Kim Il-Sung and Kim Jong-Il, trying to make amends and accusing yourself of dilettantism if you happen to be the target of criticism. After that, everyone has to read the official press or the works of Kim Il-Sung and Kim Jong-Il. This exhausting ritual, which can last as long as an hour, is part of the day-to-day life of all the inhabitants of the country, every day, without exception, in all the work units. On Saturday, there is a similar session, but longer, called 'weekly criticism'. Three distinct groups meet separately: the members of the Workers' Party, the *jingming* (retired, non-members), and the *sarochong* (the young people).

As a rule, in each of these three groups the participants are encouraged to denounce their fellow workers. If a serious breach of discipline is mentioned during one of these sessions it is referred to the hierarchy. The file of a person accused of 'liberalism' can be judged by the Party officials, who decide if the 'bad element' can or can't be 're-educated'. If he is judged 'beyond re-education', he is put in the hands of the security services and sent to a penal labour colony along with his immediate family. If the crime is redeemable in the eyes of the cadres, the guilty man is then sent – alone, without his family – to a camp devoted to re-education through labour for a variable period, depending on his social origin and his family ancestry. The more 'bourgeois' his origins, or if he has family in South Korea, the more severe the punishment. If, on the other hand, he is able to demonstrate connections with Kim Il-Sung or Kim Jong-Il (a letter of thanks obtained after giving gifts to the 'Great Leader', for example), the sentence will be less harsh. In all cases, the condemned man, if he ever returns from his stay in the camp, is physically marked by his ordeal.*

Departures for the re-education colonies, which I shall talk about later on because my father was sent to one for a time, take place collectively, at fixed dates. Every town has one. That gives you an idea of how widespread the practice is. The sentences are usually for six months, and are renewable. Each prisoner is re-evaluated after the first six months: if his attitude is judged to be bad, a more serious punishment can be meted out to him, or even a prison sentence.

---

*See Appendix, 'The Penal Labour Colonies of North Korea'.

The most stigmatised social category is that of the descendants of the 'land-owners' who existed before the foundation of the People's Democratic Republic of Korea in 1948. Next in line come the members of families of South Korean soldiers who were taken prisoner during the Korean War (1950–3). One of my father's childhood friends found himself in that situation as his father had fought with the South Korean army. He was one of the most brilliant pupils in his class, but even so, he was never allowed to go to university, or to join the army. Of all the social categories, those subject to the most serious discrimination are the families of traitors sentenced during the Korean War. There is also a great deal of suspicion about citizens with family in South Korea or Japan. Discrimination also severely afflicts the families of criminals under common law. Then there are the families of those condemned for listening to radio broadcasts from South Korea, or those who have been found in possession of South Korean books: that particular political crime is unforgivable. The guilty parties are generally brought before a firing squad, or sent to penal labour colonies for very long periods, twenty or thirty years. I learned that from my father, who spent a long time talking to one such 'criminal' during his stay in the camp.

All these pariah categories, which run into double figures and are therefore hard to list, are considered to be disloyal to

Kim Il-Sung and Kim Jong-Il and hence they don't belong to what is called the 'people'. Highest up on the ladder of the social hierarchy in North Korea are the 'members of the people', beginning with those families with a blank police file; they are called the 'clean judicial cases'. Close to the top of the pile you will find families who work 'at the centre', which is to say the employees of the Pyongyang government. It's from this fish tank of privileged categories that future cadres are taken. Finally, there are the families of Kim Il-Sung's old comrades who fought in the war against Japan. The children of this powerful caste are automatically destined to become high-ranking officials. Whatever their abilities, they will go to university. But, as with everyone else, let one member of their clan fall into criminal activity or political crime and the whole family will be relegated to a lower class. This doesn't apply to the children of cadres, who are able to plead their good social origin and generally escape camp or prison. On the other hand, those who belong to lower castes almost always see their sentences increased.

For the Party, all that counts is the degree of a person's usefulness. This political criterion is applied to everything. Even machines are awarded prizes and medals according to the same principle! This notion of 'usefulness' has a harsh effect on the fate of the handicapped. They're deported from the large cities, often at birth. Consequently, they all live in rural areas. People with physical or mental handicaps, hunchbacks, the blind, deaf mutes, they are all looked after by their families because there are no specialist institutions available. They're seen as sub-humans, useless to society, and no one speaks to them in the street. This attitude, moulded by the propaganda which puts them at the bottom of the social ladder, is very widespread. I particularly remember some neighbours who looked after their young mentally handicapped son very lovingly. One day, one of the boy's uncles came from the city with a view to subjecting him to euthanasia. The child's parents refused to let him do it, and in the end he left. Perhaps he thought that having a handicapped relative compromised his career or, more simply, brought dishonour on his whole family.

Everyone's *tsongbun* (social category) files are constantly updated. Extremely detailed, they are kept in the hands of the security services, and you can't consult them yourself. This rule has been relaxed because of the level of chaos produced by the famine. The rations that used to be supplied by the distribution system, when it still worked, were in theory the same for the different social categories. But in reality they varied according to the kind of work carried out: a manual job was preferable to the work of an accountant.

Segregation according to ancestry affects every area of

life, from work to marriage. Generally, the Party only permits marriages between people of similar or comparable
categories. An exception was made for my parents: my
mother is the daughter of a 'poor peasant' – a rather well-
regarded category – while my father is in a much less
favourable category, those who have family in Japan.

2

My Family

Boat number 48

My paternal grandfather was one of the privileged ones.
His house, which was five rows away from ours, was at least
three times as big as my parents' house. It was a building
given to him specially by the State. It abutted a plot of land
that was part of the allotted perimeter. This plot was at least
ten times as big as everyone else's. My grandparents grew
cucumbers, melons, cabbages, aubergines, courgettes,
maize, beans, turnips . . . You entered the house through a
smart wooden door reinforced by sheet metal and fitted
with a lock. I'm being specific about this because in the
other houses the doors, made of poor-quality wood, closed
with a simple padlock. This door was between the kitchen
and a storage space full of things that my grandparents had

brought from Japan. They had a television, a hi-fi and a tape recorder in one of their bedrooms. That was where all three of us slept under quilts when I came to join them. Another room was my grandfather's office, which he let me use to do my homework.

At my grandparents' house, everything was bigger than it was everywhere else: the kitchen had four fireplaces, and all the rooms were more spacious and more brightly lit because each of them had two windows. But, like all the other houses, it had an outside toilet: a wooden shack with a big hole. The excrement was regularly collected as manure for the vegetable garden.

It was at my grandparents' house that I kept my most precious possession: a collection of songs that I illustrated myself and bound with thread and cardboard. I spent days and days making it, very carefully. Some of the songs were of my own devising, mocking versions of official odes. Here is one of them, in its original, official version:

We grow up in the land of freedom
All the little comrades march in rows
Singing in this paradise of peace
Tell me, what can the world envy us?

And here is my version:

My Family

They sell apples in the land of freedom
Let our grandparents munch on them as they break their
* backs*
Come on, grandad, with your rotten teeth
You won't? An old man who isn't hungry? What a fool.

I also composed a variation of the song in a film by Kim Jong-Il, released in 1990, which is part of a big saga on the Korean War entitled *The Destiny of the People*. I no longer remember the original version, but here is the parody I wrote:

I went to beg a bowl of rice from my poor parents-in-law.
But in vain, because they turned me away. And now that
the state food distributions are gone we realise how precious
a simple bowl of rice can be. Oh, that's a lesson I never
will forget.

Of course, I never showed the collection to anyone, except to my three best friends: Choljin, Kuanyok and Kuanjin.

My paternal grandparents loved me very much, particularly my grandmother, who wanted me to stay with her. So, when I was nine, my parents took me to live with my grandparents. I was happier living there, because it was the loveliest house in the whole of Onsong. The walls

25

were whitewashed, and the roof was covered with good-quality brown tiles that gleamed in the sun. Even the Secretary of the Workers' Party didn't live in such a beautiful place!

The reason the authorities treated my paternal grandparents so benevolently was simple. Previously they had lived in Japan, like many Koreans. Back when the Korean peninsula was a Japanese colony (1910–45), hundreds of thousands of Koreans had been deported to Japan as forced labourers.* Later, thousands more Koreans, fleeing the Korean War, joined them in the Japanese archipelago. This happened to be the case with my father's family who, although originally from South Korea, found refuge in Japan at that time. Then, in the late fifties, following the example of tens of thousands of other pro-Communist Koreans, almost all the members of my family chose to return and settle in North Korea, and turned their goods over to the Communist regime.

At that time, many people were returning to the country. Grandfather told me that for several years dozens of boats had been chartered to ferry all the 'patriotic' families that had been encouraged to come back to Korea by the *Chosen*

---

*From the annexation of Korea by Japan, in 1910 until 1945, some two million one hundred thousand Koreans were deported to Japan as forced labourers.

Soren, Japan's pro-Communist Korean association.* The slogan at the time was 'Let's go home'. Being very patriotic, some members of my paternal father's family finally made their minds up to do just that. Twelve of them arrived in North Korea in 1960. That story has been recounted to me so many times! There was my grandfather, my grandmother, my great-grandparents, a great-uncle, a great-aunt and her husband, as well as four uncles and an aunt.

The ships repatriating the Koreans carried thousands of passengers. Many a time when they evoked these memories my grandparents told me how they had found themselves on boat number 48. They arrived at Chongjin, where some functionaries in charge of allocations assigned them, without giving them any choice, a job and a house in the city of Onsong. My father was born there shortly afterwards.

Life was hard from the very start, especially since we are a large family. My father told me that they lived mostly on

---

* The *Chosen Soren*, set up in Japan in 1955 to repatriate Koreans to the Communist North, began a 'going home' programme in 1959. It had one weighty ally: the International Red Cross. Thousands of Koreans from Japan applied, and signed with their eyes closed. The programme was interrupted by the Japanese government in 1967 because of suspicions about the way repatriated people were treated in North Korea. But, thanks to the support of politicians in Japan, the *Chosen Soren* managed to re-establish the link in 1971. In total, between 1959 and 1984, at the end of 187 sea voyages, 93,339 Koreans were repatriated in this way – to their great misfortune.

soup, rarely on meat. Everyone expressed their regrets about leaving Japan almost immediately. From a very young age, my father heard his parents complaining about the wretched conditions of life in North Korea. 'When we lived so well in Japan . . .' grandfather would always say. Their regret was intensified by the fact that at the time of their departure, the *Chosen Soren* had told them not to take anything with them, saying that they would find 'everything you need there'. In fact, there was nothing in North Korea. A good thing my grandmother had packed a few plates and pans! The quality of utensils that were to be found in Onsong was so dreadful that that precious cooking equipment brought back from Japan in 1960 lasted us the whole of our stay, right up until we fled.

To thank 'patriotic families' like ours Kim Il-Sung had, nonetheless, granted them certain privileges. For my grandparents that favour came in the form of a particularly fine house. The Great Leader also sent them gifts from time to time. These might have been bottles of *taepyeung sul*, a very expensive rice spirit that most people can't afford, or else sweets or cakes. The special favours that my grandparents enjoyed were also explained – or perhaps particularly explained – by the fact that one of my great-uncles, who runs a major company in Japan, had been very generous towards the Popular Democratic Republic of Korea in the seventies. He was part of the *Chosen Soren*, which he did, however, finally leave in disgust, after learning the truth about our living conditions. But I only understood that much later, after we had fled the country.

The most bitter of all was my grandfather. 'We were deceived,' he repeated constantly, taking care, of course, that no one outside of the family could hear him. My grandmother did all she could to get him to be quiet: 'You're mad! Don't say that! Do you want us to end our days in a penal labour colony? Think of us and the children!' My grandfather was full of regret at having allowed himself to be duped. He talked to my grandmother about it in bed at night, in a low voice, of course, and in Japanese in case anyone understood. But since he now lived in North Korea and it was impossible to leave, he tried to win the favour of the Great Leader so that he could live as well as possible. To thank Kim Il-Sung for granting him a comfortable place to live, he sent the Generalissimo Head of State some *nogyong* (doe horns), which Koreans crush and consume to give themselves strength. He bought them with the money given to us by the rest of our family who had stayed in Japan. That precious money did a great deal to improve our everyday lives, particularly at the start of the famine. After that had run out we starved, like everyone else.

It was only after our escape to China that my father told me all this. Before that I had only ever had a vague idea of how things really were. I had somehow sensed that there was a profound dissatisfaction at the heart of the family, a kind of sly dissidence that floated above our heads like a storm cloud. But as far as I was concerned that was an additional reason to repress those feelings, which hinted at unhappiness and death. I took refuge in what I was taught at school, because that seemed much more reassuring for a child like me. Kim Jong-Il, 'Beloved Dear Leader, Great General, clear-sighted and invincible . . .' I was all the more willing to believe in all this because my father, wishing to protect me, as he later confessed, went to great efforts to do so by censoring everything that wasn't orthodox – whether it was my grandfather's rages, or details of everyday life that happened to contradict the official slogans. He sidestepped anything that might have given me doubts, he banished it from my sight. It was a question of survival, not just for me, but for the whole family. So he set about making me *sincerely* orthodox, the kind of person who acted like a good son of the Party.

That didn't stop me writing my parody songs. I felt, subconsciously, that something was wrong.

The mine

My father was a miner. The mine, which had been in use since the forties, was more than one hundred metres underground. There were tracks in the galleries, with wagons and all kinds of extracting machinery running on them. My father worked with a lamp powered by a two-kilo battery attached to his belt. It was in the miners' rest-room, hung with portraits of the two Kims, that the political study sessions took place. The portraits of the two Kims also decorated the galleries, and were protected by a wooden frame and a plate of glass. All through the mine there were instructive slogans painted on banners, such as 'What the Party decides, we accomplish', 'Whether it be production, political studies or daily life, everything must be accomplished as vigorously as a battle against the Japanese occupying forces', 'Do not leave before fulfilling your quotas', 'Let us give our lives to protect Comrade Great Leader Kim Il-Sung', 'Let us build socialist paradise on earth' . . .

When my mother was young, she worked in the mine as well. She drove an electric railcar that pulled the wagons. After she married she was obliged to leave her much coveted driver's job to someone else. Although it may have been just as well that she did so, because the mine was dangerous. There were hundreds of galleries underground, some of them seven hundred metres long. Fire-damp explosions and collapses were frequent, because the wooden struts propping up the galleries were often stolen by people who sold them for food. The mine was plunged into mourning on average once a month. Accidental injuries were also very common. The work unit's hospital took charge of everything on such occasions, but its methods were pretty basic. Amputation was the general rule, and medication was still impossible to find. Hewers, drivers, carpenters: two hundred miners worked in the pit. Two thousand eight hundred people were employed in sorting and other ancillary tasks. The miners were the best paid – one hundred and ten wons a month, as opposed to seventy to eighty for the mine cadres.

Kim Jong-Il sometimes issued instructions called 'battle orders'. When he did this my father was paid double his salary: two hundred and twenty wons. But it meant that the whole mine had to speed up production for two hundred days in a row. This was men's work! So a number of times my father spent a month or even two in the mine without ever coming out. He had to do twice as much work as usual, and sleep in dormitories set up in the galleries. No one left the mines until the quotas of extracted coal had been fulfilled. When my father finally did emerge, dirty and tired, his eyes could no longer bear the light of day. After one particular 'battle order', the chief overseer told him to take ten days' rest. But my father refused, accepting a break of only forty-eight hours. His Stakhanovite zeal was explained by the fact that he had a goal in mind: to get himself noticed and win a medal as a model worker, with a view to becoming a member of the Workers' Party. Membership of the Party is indispensable for any kind of social promotion, such as to the posts of cadre and the privileges attached to them. And a Party man, when he walks in the street, is always saluted by everyone, called 'comrade' and treated with respect.

But my father never did manage to join the Party, because he had a reputation for getting into scraps. Twice, in the eighties, he had for that reason been subjected to 'comrade trials'. These are public courts where suspects arrested for anti-social crimes are brought before crowds of hundreds of people. In Onsong, the sessions generally take place in a large square reserved for ceremonies, or in the mine's 'great hall of culture'. The accused are lined up on a platform and they have their charges read to them. The assembled throng is then asked by the police cadres to judge whether a particular person should be expelled from the city, or whether he should instead be pardoned. Those expelled are relegated to the countryside, to very subordinate and tiresome jobs. The first time this happened, my father and his friends had fought another group of hooligans with spades and axes. Quite a few of them had been injured. And again the second time, in about 1988, he had delivered a severe beating to two guys from a rival gang. Both times, my father had escaped the worst. But he was a marked man nonetheless. He was the only man in his family to live outside the Party – apart from his younger brother. It wasn't that his brother had the same fighting temperament, but he was automatically proscribed because of an internal Party rule stipulating that a person can only claim to join the ranks if his elders are there already. This principle is summed up in a maxim: 'Water always flows downhill . . .' My paternal grandmother wasn't a member of the Party either, but that was for a different reason. It is actually much easier for a man to obtain a Party card than it is for a woman, who has to make more effort than a male competitor. According to my father, only about one per cent of women joined the Party, while one man in ten was a member.

My grandparents, who also worked in the mine like the rest of the family, had additional sources of income that proved to be indispensable after the start of the famine, in about 1993. They raised pigs that they sold individually on the free market. They also owned cats and dogs that they ended up selling on the market to make a bit of money. Were they eaten by the people who bought them? I don't know . . . I also remember a goat, which my grandparents used to make medicinal potions. They had a great belief, like everyone else, in the virtues of these mixtures, called *yomso yot* (goat sweets), which they made by boiling up caramel with goat meat. In Onsong, it is said to be very good for

While the pupils hoed, sowed or harvested, they were washed with a continuous flow of revolutionary songs. These were always very cheerful. They were broadcast by a propaganda lorry equipped with enormous loudspeakers

The schoolmaster, his hand always ready to deliver a thrashing, laid into me so fiercely that day that I lost count of the blows

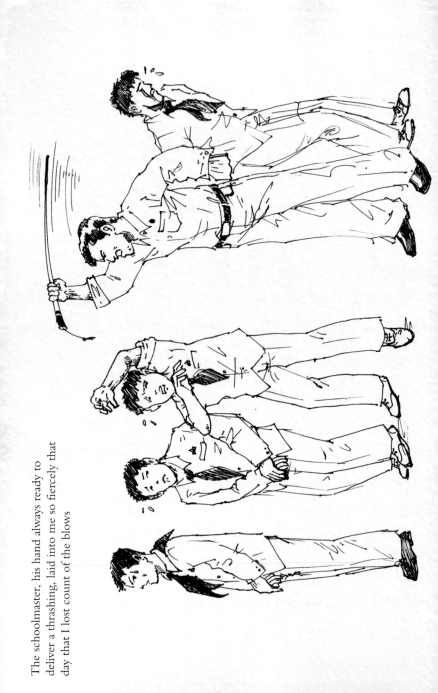

Me and my three best friends, Choljin, Kuanyok and Kuanjin.
We were inseparable from secondary school onwards

The famine took its toll. As time passed there were fewer and fewer of us sitting at the school desks

Lots of hungry children steal from Onsong market

Onsong station was filled with people waiting for trains that never came. Skeletal children wandered about the waiting room

During the famine, everyone thought only of himself. Corpses were sometimes left exposed for a whole day. No one stopped to take notice

On 9 March 1998, we had crossed the river border that separated us from China. I fought my way among the blocks of ice. The soldiers who were chasing us called to us to come back

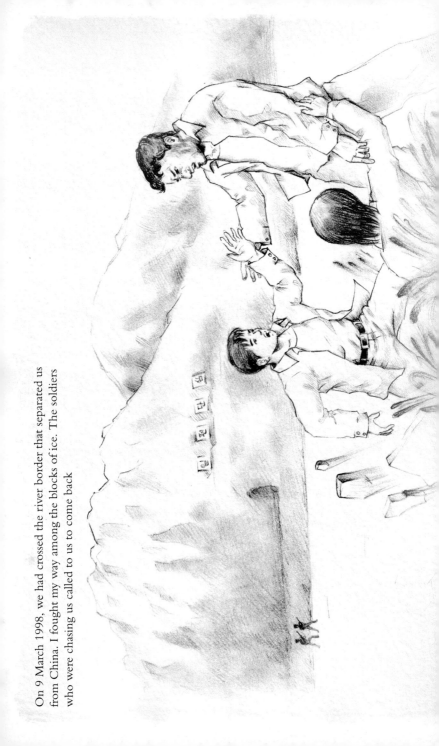

the sick and for people with weak constitutions. Obviously, when you don't eat your fill in normal times you need a tonic of some kind! Weak people are also fed a health-giving concoction consisting of stuffed chicken with sticky rice and ginseng. Dog meat is also highly prized. I've eaten it several times, but only on special occasions, because it's very expensive. But once I did have some because I'd been bitten by a dog. There's a saying that to avoid dying from a dog-bite, you've got to eat some dog meat. To kill the animal, people hang it from a tree and let it die of strangulation. Sometimes it's drowned in a sack, but that's not so common. People also eat cats which, like goats, often end up in medicinal potions. My grandmother told me that she fell ill when she was small, so her father decided to kill a cat to help her regain her strength. He plunged the living animal into a pot of boiling water and put the lid on. But the cat managed to get its head out, and miaowed and miaowed and finally died with its head wedged under the lid, casting desperate glances that frightened the life out of grandma.

My grandfather was a very quiet man who spent most of his time reading. His mother tongue was Japanese, which he spoke perfectly. He could speak Korean, but had trouble spelling it, and tended to write it phonetically. Nonetheless, he was a perfectionist. Everything had to be impeccable as far as he was concerned. His vegetable garden was exemplary, everything perfectly aligned, not a single weed. When he did the housework at home there wasn't a speck of dust in sight. Even my grandmother wasn't as maniacal about cleanliness. I remember he liked drinking *soju*. He ate a lot of sweets, just as I did. But grandfather was very severe when I was a child. To his great despair, I always had a rebellious streak. He was forever lecturing me, but I didn't listen to him. When he gave me a severe talking to, I went and hid in my grandmother's skirts, because I was her pet.

Sparrow kebabs

North Koreans start drinking and smoking very early. I myself started puffing on cigarettes at the age of eight. The first time it happened I stole my grandfather's cigarettes from the wooden box he kept them in. Then, to smoke them, I hid with two friends behind the maize stalks that the reapers arranged in stacks after the harvest, in the autumn. They look like little tents, open at the top. As my friends and I lit up one cigarette after another, smoke escaped through the opening and my grandfather discovered us . . . I got a good hiding for that.

I used to do some pretty stupid things. One day I was standing with my hands in my pockets watching a neighbour burning weeds. Noticing that I had time on my hands, he asked me to keep an eye on the fire while he went away for a moment, asking me to take special care because his house wasn't very far from the flames. I agreed and he left. But it was lunchtime, and when my grand-mother called me in, like an idiot I left the fire untended. As I ate my maize porridge, I heard our neighbours crying, 'Fire!' Through the window I saw that the flames had reached the stable where an ox was kept. This was a very serious business. The neighbour accused me of carelessness. I tried to lie my way out of it, saying that he hadn't asked me to keep an eye on the fire, but deep down I felt terri-bly guilty. My grandfather gave me a very severe reprimand and I fled to my parents' house. But after a few days I went back to my grandparents. They had forgiven me . . . They really did love me a lot. My parents weren't offended by the fact that I preferred to stay with my grandparents. They often came to visit us, because we lived very close to one another.

I was unruly from nursery school onwards. Once I threw a big stone into the playground, shouting that it was a grenade. I thought everyone would throw themselves on the ground the way they did in the war films we were shown, or in the martial arts stories we were given to read. Not a bit of it. One pupil caught the stone full in the face. I tackled a little girl who was running to report me to the teacher, threatening that I would 'kill her on the spot' if she did. But some other pupils ratted on me, and I got a sound thrashing. The teacher, who was handy with a clip around the ear, gave me I don't know how many blows of the cane on the calves that day. And the victim's mother came to beat me as well. What a terrible time that was!

I often went to play 'Korean War' in the galleries of the mines with my friends. The mountain is riddled with them, though it's dangerous to venture into the abandoned galleries. They are no longer properly supported, and children have been known to die in rock falls. We divided up into two 'armies', the 'bastard imperialist Americans' on one side (the weakest among us were always chosen for that role) and the stout North Korean soldiers on the other. We plunged into the black holes, not carrying torches or anything. Most of the time we were in total darkness, whispering to one another, ambushing our enemies, plotting surprise attacks. The fact of our being in a group did nothing to lessen the fear that we felt in those dark, cold, damp passageways, our hearts thumping in our ears.

We also used to hang about at a rubbish dump not far from Onsong that received mountains of waste from France, where we found all kinds of wrappings, supermarket bags, disposable razors, toothpaste tubes – and particularly plastic bottles. From the nineties onwards, whole cartloads were regularly dumped there. They were designed to be recycled. Using that raw material, a little factory working on a coal heater produced plastic sheets that were used to cover greenhouses. But anyone could help themselves. So we brought home mineral water bottles, which came in very handy.

Our games also took us to the river, where there were whirlpools. In the winter we pushed each other around on the ice on little sledges. But we were often much more troublesome than that. The military atmosphere in which we were brought up stressed the martial ideas of heroism and temerity. The most daring of us were Yongjin and Kyongjin. Particularly Kyongjin, who impressed us by jumping from the roofs of the houses. Sometimes he hurt himself, but he started over again anyway. They were good friends. We were together all the time because we had always lived in the same neighbourhood. Sometimes we went and set fire to the fields! It's very easy in the winter as everything's so dry. There were seven or eight of us that got together, and we really enjoyed doing that. We knew that it was forbidden, as fire can wreak havoc to great stretches of land, and even lay waste a whole village. That kind of thing had happened in the past. But even so, we carried on regardless. Fire was one of our few distractions. I used to tiptoe out of the house at night to meet up with friends who were waiting for me in the fields to play with flaming torches. It's called *hepulori*: you hold the torch at arm's length and spin it around very quickly, making glowing circles. We pretended we were at war, and played at being soldiers sending signals. We also played at seeing who was bravest, rolling in a campfire. Sometimes I came home with my clothes half charred!

One of my favourite pastimes consisted of flushing out sparrows from roof tiles. My mates and I would climb up on to the roofs of houses and factories. This put the rows of tiles out of alignment, and we used to get a real earful from the grown-ups. Not at the time, but during the monsoon, because when it rained the water used to get in between the disjointed tiles. When we did this at the factories, which had bigger roofs, we often came back with whole sacks of baby birds. I used to bring them to my grandmother, who threw them, still alive, to the two pigs she was fattening up. 'That'll make good pork!' she said. And we needed pork when the famine came. Pork and sparrows, because when we were really hungry, my friends and I, we couldn't keep from making some tasty kebabs out of the little birds. We lit a fire, gutted the baby birds, impaled them on bicycle spokes, and cooked them, gorging ourselves.

The first time I ate chocolate was when I was five years old. I wasn't to have the chance to do that again until we escaped to China, years later. Our great-uncles and great-aunts who had stayed in Japan had been given exceptional permission to visit us. They came like extraterrestrials, with their arms full of presents and food. They gave each adult a small amount of money and a Seiko watch with rubies. They brought me a bear costume that slipped on like a boiler suit, with holes for the eyes and paws at the ends of the arms and legs. When you pressed the bear's nose, it sang a Japanese lullaby. I looked utterly ridiculous in it. I remember our neighbours being so tormented by curiosity that they pressed their noses up against our windows, looking at me in my weird get-up, their eyes wide with astonishment. And my great-uncles and great-aunts had brought me five of those costumes, with the heads of different animals!

I also remember waving tins of condensed milk and chocolate bars under my friends' noses and provoking them: 'You'd like some of this, wouldn't you! Well catch it if you can!' I was a horrid little boy. I didn't yet know what famine was.

Windows on the outside world

My great-aunts had also brought a colour television from Japan. This meant that we were incredibly lucky, since on average only one family in ten had a television, and almost all of them were black and white. From that point onwards, the whole village came to watch television at our house. About thirty people would pile into my grandparents' house almost every evening, with children at the front and grown-ups at the back; and at least as many poked their heads through the windows to be sure they didn't miss any of the spectacle!

In North Korea there's only one channel, which broadcasts revolutionary operas, revolutionary series, Soviet revolutionary films and movies of the day about ancient Korean heroes who stole from the rich to give to the poor. I particularly remember *Mission 0-27*, a film glorifying the sacrifice of the special North Korean forces who had infiltrated South Korea to assassinate the 'puppet', President Park Chun-Hee. In actual fact, the mission failed, but in the film the death of the commando unit is presented as a dazzling patriotic success. One of the soldiers blows himself up with a hand-grenade in a helicopter, while another crashes his plane into the South Korean battleship *Wolmido*.

Anyway, as a general rule, the last moments of cinema heroes are always presented in a very stereotypical way. In *Fast as Thunder and Lightning*, another squad of special forces secretly enters the South on the joint orders of Kim Il-Sung and Kim Jong-Il. As in *Mission 0-27*, they too perish at the end of the film, clearly articulating in their final death rattle the words: 'Long live the Great Leader Ruling Comrade and Generalissimo Kim Il-Sung and the Dear Leader Comrade Kim Jong-Il, and long live the People's Democratic Republic of Korea!' Some of them even had the strength to add, for the benefit of the surviving soldiers: 'I leave you with the task of saving our country and our people.'

As we were quite close to the Chinese border, we were able to pick up the Beijing channels. That was totally and utterly forbidden, but we did it anyway, at night, with the curtains drawn. Chinese television gave us an absolutely incredible view of the world. There were cars everywhere, rich people who ate all the time and delicious-looking food, buildings that looked like mirrors, lovely homes piled high with household appliances and electric gadgets. That said, we were suspicious of these pictures, because North Korean television also produced pseudo-documentaries that showed us as prosperous and happy, which we certainly weren't. Was this the same kind of artificial propaganda? I heard my parents wondering about that. Chinese television looked a hundred times truer than our one channel though.

One of the most surprising things for us to see was actors kissing each other on the lips. There was none of that in our films of revolutionary comradeship! In our country, the steamiest you got was a slight embrace, sometimes with the model male worker patting the shoulder of the meritorious female worker.

Two of my father's friends who were in the police force used to drop by in secret to take a look at the Chinese broadcasts. But as a general rule we had to keep all the forbidden things we saw on television strictly to ourselves. The slightest reference, the slightest word could have given us away. If that had happened, our whole family would have risked being deported to the special penal labour colonies, the ones you never come back from.

When a family is condemned, the men in the security services* sometimes snap up three whole generations: the grandparents, the great-uncles and the great-aunts, all the way down to the grandchildren and cousins. That happened to one of our neighbours. Having said that, if any problems like that had arisen, dad and granddad might have been able to make use of the letters that the secretariat of Kim Il-Sung and Kim Jong-Il had sent to thank them for the presents they had given. Letters like that generally reduce serious sentences. But an anti-socialist crime remains an anti-socialist crime and, in the best possible case, my father would have been condemned to at least six months in Onsong's penal labour colony, where he had every chance of dying of hunger or exhaustion. For fear that I might absentmindedly divulge something or other, my parents and grandparents kept me from watching the

---

*There are two kinds of police. At a local level, the Department of Popular Security (*Inmin Boanseong*) and, on the national scale, the Department of National Security (*Kukga Bowibu*).

forbidden channels. And they kept me from singing forbidden songs, unaware that, rebellious boy that I was, I
was writing them myself.

Only the hymns dedicated to Kim Il-Sung and Kim
Jong-Il were permitted, only they were broadcast. But even
so, my grandmother had taught me some nursery rhymes
in Japanese, without mum and dad's knowledge. I was only
able to hum them at home, or in secret.

On my birthday I didn't have presents or songs. But to
mark the occasion my mother cooked rice rather than
maize porridge. On New Year's Day and at weddings, on
the other hand, people enjoyed themselves and sang a lot.
Tables were set up outside and all the invited neighbours
ate, drank and partied. The celebrations lasted all night. At
these banquets there was generally fish, pig's head, tripe
sausage and sweet rice noodles. During the famine, that
kind of indulgence was greatly reduced. There were fewer
guests, less food, and the lady of the house collected the
leftovers and sold them at the market the next day. But even
so, it wasn't a day like any other. Having a party was an
opportunity to forget everyday life and to sing your head
off. We Koreans love to sing.

The first South Korean tune to reach my ears came
from a propaganda film about the assassination of Park
Chun-Hee. In that fiction, the South Korean President

hummed a tune that was popular in the South, just before he died. I had been seduced by that 'puppet' song, and I wasn't alone. Many people hummed it furtively, and even some of the musicians in the orchestra at the mine had a go at it. The ditty became so popular that it was specifically forbidden. In 1988, my father told me, a Party secretary in Onsong who had had the foolish idea of singing it all the way through after a boozy banquet was expelled from the Party for that reason, and demoted back to the rank of simple worker. Mozart, Beethoven and Chopin were off-limits as well. But my father, a great music lover, had managed to get hold of some European classical music cassettes from China, and even recordings of South Korean and Japanese songs. He listened to them at home after closing all the doors and windows. Mum told him off every time, warning him that it was far too dangerous. And sure enough, one day, a security agent turned up at our house when dad and some of his cousins were dancing to forbidden music. The agent demanded the cassette. But my father turned as nice as pie, and offered him a whole pack of Sony cassettes of North Korean music. He accepted, and didn't report us. But it was a close shave! Immediately after the man left, my father collected all the compromising tapes and put them in a safe hiding-place, for fear that he might come back and confiscate them. It didn't happen . . . And that's worth pointing out, because his kind of attitude was rather rare.

In North Korea everyone is suspicious of everyone else, all the time. There are security spies in every work unit, but you never know who they are, or how many. And they spy on each other as well. My father, who worked in the mine as part of a team of seventy miners, thought he had spotted at least three or four. But there's no way of being completely certain. The comrade you trust, the one who always comes to see you at your house in the evening, may very easily turn out to be a clever security agent. There is, on the other hand, no mutual espionage within the family cell. The family is considered to be an indivisible unit, and 'collectively responsible'.

Meals for the dead

On important feast days, such as the birthdays of Kim Il-Sung and Kim Jong-Il, the office of food distribution, while it was still in operation, sometimes allowed us a bottle of spirits, a handful of sweets and some biscuits. The biscuits were so hard that you couldn't eat them just like that. You first had to soften them in boiling water. As I've said, in normal times the office distributed very small portions of crushed maize and rice. We kept a little aside for special occasions. For example for *Hanshikil*, the Day of the Dead,

5 April, and for the anniversaries of the deaths of close relations.

On *Hanshikil*, all the inhabitants go to Mount Namsan, at ten o'clock on the dot, where the dead are buried. Everyone dresses in black except the children. Lots of people cry and wail at the top of their voices. There's an incredible crowd – from a distance it's pretty impressive to see all those black patches trekking up the hill, like soldiers taking a mountain. Up there, poor people have only a wooden stele, while the more wealthy, such as the Party cadres, pay for stone, even marble.

All classes mingle to respect this ancestor-cult. To my great-grandparents' grave we brought a basket full of food; grilled tofu, bottles of spirits and fruit placed on plates in arrangements of three. All of this food was generally prepared the previous day by the women of the family, who did the cooking together. Sometimes they worked through the night.

Having reached the graveside, we each prostrated ourselves three times, pressing our foreheads to the ground. Then we 'fed' the dead, putting a piece of each dish in a bowl of rice placed by the gravestone, in a hole dug in the ground. Grandfather poured spirits into the bowl and around the grave. As he did so he spoke to the dead, asking them to grant us more blessings: 'We have spent this year well, thanks to you, but life is getting harder and

harder, take greater care of us, give us a better life . . .'
Then a spoon was stuck into the rice so that the dead
could eat.

This ceremony was performed by every member of the
family. Each gesture had to be repeated three times because
the number three is the number of the dead. Grandfather
also lit a cigarette, which he placed on a tray so that our
loved ones could have a smoke. Then, all together by the
graveside, we ate what remained of the offerings, which
were called 'blessed food', although we didn't touch the
food of the dead.

When I was little, I found it very curious that the food
of the dead disappeared from one year to the next. I
thought the dead really were eating it. I later discovered
that it was wild animals who emptied the bowls of offerings. After the death of my grandfather, we neglected my
great-grandfather's grave at Mount Namsan to go to
Kokosan, where grandfather was buried. It was closer to
our house, and less exhausting to get to. The side of the hill
reserved for the dead faced towards the east, where the sun
rises, which is a good omen.

When the famine began to make its presence felt, many
inhabitants lacked the resources to prepare all the necessary
dishes. Subsequently, some families were almost decimated
by hunger; even if they had food to give to the dead, sur-
vivors of the famine didn't have the strength to climb the

mountain up to the cemetery. And besides, many didn't even have the energy to bury their dead, so the task was often performed by neighbours who were still in reasonable health. At this point the number of graves began to multiply, and you would often see the graves of grandparents, parents, uncles, aunts and children, all lined up and bearing dates clustered very close together.

My grandparents, though they were quite well-off, suffered from hunger from the very beginning of the restrictions. In 1993 they were, like my parents, reduced to consuming nothing but maize porridge. That year they were forbidden to communicate with the Japanese side of the family. The authorities suspended all mail abroad, so that the outside world would know nothing of the famine. This meant that the money orders stopped coming in as well, and my grandparents found themselves for the first time without a penny. My grandfather, who was used to good Japanese food, couldn't digest the food substitutes he was obliged to choke down. He stopped eating, and finally died of weakness in 1994, the same year as Kim Il-Sung. He was constantly asking for meat, which had become very scarce. We managed to find him some, and my grandmother prepared him a meal. Immediately after eating it he died, just like that, all of a sudden.

3

'The Child Is the Future of the Party and the Nation'

Uniforms

To get to school I had to cross a bridge over a river. Classes were held in a series of buildings on street level arranged into two sections, primary and secondary. In each classroom there hung, of course, a photograph of Kim Il-Sung and another of Kim Jong-Il, side by side. These pictures were very large, and placed just above the blackboard so that we could always see them, which gave us the impression that the rulers' eyes were on us at all times. We knew by heart every feature of their smooth faces, just as we knew the slogans that we were taught: 'We will fight the puppet party of South Korea'; 'What the Party decides, we will put into practice', 'For the Great Leader, let us become

51

human bullets and bombs to protect him with all our determination', 'Let us resolutely defend Kim Jong-Il', 'Let us
reunite our fatherland', 'A hundred battles, a hundred vic-
tories', 'Every Korean is worth one hundred enemies',
'Military service for the fatherland and the people' . . .

We learned dozens of songs of a similar vein: 'The bay-
onet gleams, and our footsteps echo, we are soldiers of the
great general . . . Who could withstand us? We shine with
fine assurance, we are the army of the comrade leader.' I
was taught that song at the age of ten and I still know it by
heart. I remember the soldiers singing it at Kim Il-Sung's
birthday celebrations in Pyongyang. When they were
shown on television, I joined in loudly. I also hummed it all
the time because it often slipped into my head without my
realising it, and once I started I couldn't stop, I had to go on
to the final chorus.

At the back of the classroom there was a panel showing
the list of pupils on cleaning duty, the list of the best pupils,
the best marks, the pupils whose 'level of morality' was
high and those who, like me, wouldn't stop doing silly
things, who chattered in class, didn't bother reporting on
the others, who neglected cleaning duties or forgot to do
their homework. A chart, which changed every week,
listed those children who were considered to be 'good' or
'bad examples'. A phrase in bold script warned the latter
that they had to 'change their behaviour', while the former

were urged to 'continue with their behaviour'. The panel
was completed with a poem to the glory of Kim Il-Sung
and his 'much-loved' son, and a fashionable song on the
same theme. A poem or a song could not be considered
satisfactory, our teacher said, if the Great Leader or the
Dear Leader were not mentioned in it. For us, it gradually
became unthinkable that any kind of artistic work could be
produced without the two Kims at its centre. In actual fact,
it was even forbidden to sing a song or write a poem that
didn't mention the two Kims at some point or other.

In the North Korean school system, nursery school,
where you start learning to read and write, is followed by
four years of primary and six of secondary school. After
that, everyone joins the army for thirteen years of compulsory military service.* You leave military service at the age
of thirty, and it's only then that you can start thinking about
girls and marriage. Most of us, from a very young age, had
no desire to go to university. The collective ideal was
entirely directed towards the army and the defence of the
country against the imperialist puppet aggressors. Besides,

---

*The duration of military service for men was lowered from thir-
teen to ten years in March 2003. For girls, it has gone from ten to
seven years. Military service only lasted four years in 1958. It went
up to ten in 1993, under Kim Il-Sung, then to thirteen for men in
1996.

we were prepared for it from the second year of primary school, when we were given classes in Tae-Kwon Do. This Korean martial art was part of the basic training of the valiant soldiers of Kim Il-Sung and Kim Jong-Il. It was rumoured that just one of their fingers was enough to kill someone!

At school, we had uniforms which we were told had been given to us as a present by Kim Jong-Il. It seemed that the 'Dear Leader', at least in theory, was very attentive to children. One of his quotations, often repeated to us, compares schoolchildren to 'flower buds', which have to be tended so that they will grow, because 'children represent the treasure and the future of the nation and the Party'. Every four years, thanks to the Dear Leader, we received a summer uniform and another for the winter. These uniforms were navy blue, and cut in a military style. We put our fountain pens in our breast pockets, from which they had to show slightly. On the pocket on the side of our hearts we attached the badge of Kim Il-Sung or Kim Jong-Il. The best thing was to get hold of the badge that had come out most recently: your friends would envy you. In secondary school, we wore a cap adorned with a yellow star, the same one you see on the national flag. The girls wore skirts with black stockings. The children of poor families had less well cared-for, more worn-out uniforms.

In North Korea, a class – consisting of between thirty

and thirty-five pupils – is normally divided into *zhu* (units) of four: two boys and two girls. The *zhuzhang* (head of unit) wears an armband with a stripe and three stars. In most cases the head of unit is a girl, because the chief function of the head of unit is to clean the classroom, and boys tend to avoid that kind of duty. The *haku panzhang* (head of class) wears two red stripes and two red stars. He is chosen by the teacher for his high standards of behaviour and his sense of responsibility. The *pundan yuwon* (first in the class, or member of the section committee) has two red stripes and three stars. Three of the pupils in the class have two stars and three stripes: they are the ones who are supposed to perform 'good deeds', and the other pupils have to follow their example. What the school calls 'good deeds' consists of, among other things, showing zeal in the compulsory collection of paper for recycling, or of copper. The highest rank (three stripes and three stars) goes to the school delegate, called *duiwui wonzhan*, or head of section committee. He has almost as much power as a teacher. He can even answer back to his teachers.

But all these ranks, which are supposed to reward the best of us, conceal a completely different reality. They mask many shenanigans between teachers and the parents of pupils. Parents often bribe the teachers with small gifts or other favours to ensure the promotion of their little rascal to a higher stripe. This kind of clientelism is common practice. And invariably, the *duiwui wonzhan* is the child of a Party big shot or a well-off family. As for myself, I was from a family that was considered well-to-do, even wealthy. But as I wasn't well-behaved at school, since I didn't always do my homework and was often cheeky to teachers, I never received any rewards. When the classroom had to be decorated, I simply refused to do it and skipped class. I was very rebellious. To put it bluntly, the teachers bored the hell out of me.

One plus one is one

School usually opened its doors at 7.30 a.m. We had five forty-five-minute classes in the morning, a lunch break during which we went home to eat, then another three or four classes in the afternoon from two o'clock onwards. Some subjects were considered minor, like gymnastics (which we performed collectively to revolutionary music), Chinese and English. On the other hand, marks in mathematics, geography, the history of Korea and the Party were very important indeed. There were also morality classes, in which we were taught politeness and respect. Two subjects that we swotted up on every day were particularly choice: 'Era of childhood (I)' and 'Era of childhood (II)'. The first class dealt with the childhood of Kim Il-Sung, and the second with the childhood of his son Kim Jong-Il. We had to learn the lives of these two great men of Korea by heart, down to the smallest detail: the time Kim Il-Sung crossed the An Nok river when he went to the Soviet Union, the way he defeated the Japanese invaders in 1945 all by himself, etc. In the fourth year of primary school I learned that when he was young, Kim Il-Sung was very good at football, that he was a centre-forward, and that he was always the one who scored goals for his team. Our schoolbooks also testified, beyond the merest shadow of a doubt, to the unparalleled genius of Kim Il-Sung. Since his earliest childhood there had been no one like him at solving problems. When a teacher put the question to the class: 'There are ten birds on a branch. A hunter kills one of them, how many are left on the branch?' all the children in the class said 'nine'. Only the future head of State Great Leader Kim Il-Sung replied, 'None, because the others would have flown away.'

The same was said of his son Kim Jong-Il, whom we were told about over and over, whether it was his illustrious place of birth at the foot of Mount Paektu, the highest mountain in Korea, or his prodigious talent, even at games, which no one could beat. He was a precocious child, bubbling with intelligence and cunning, as the countless parables we were told about his life sought to demonstrate. During the war against Japan, we were told, he had thrown a big rock from the top of a mountain on to a Japanese soldier in a boat, killing him on the spot. Another legend had it that one day, when flocks of birds were cackling and chattering around the couch where his father was taking a nap between two exhausting battles, Kim Jong-Il set about chasing them. To avoid waking his brave and illustrious father, he made big and silent gestures that were enough to dispel the chirping creatures. Such intelligence! On another occasion, he had a competition with some other children where the idea was to throw a chicken feather as far as possible. He won by simply blowing on the feather, while all his rivals stupidly tried to hurl it like a stone. To convince us that Kim Junior was a formidable idealist, we were told that as a child he climbed trees in order to catch rainbows, which he finally succeeded in doing . . . A kind of demigod, then! And like all the others – even if today, with hindsight, I may give the impression of mocking it all – I can assure you that at the time I swallowed it whole. I was inspired by an unshakeable faith. Although my classmates were unaware of it, I saw reassuring lights glowing from the two Kims; they alone could light our way and improve our gloomy lives. They were fabulous, great-hearted, heroic characters without whom the 'people', all of us, were lost, destined to be cast into the darkness of death. I was convinced that it was thanks to their endless love of the fatherland that we had managed to survive this far.

I recently found one of my schoolbooks from the second year of primary school, the one about the 'Era of childhood (II)'. The cover shows the Jong-Il Peak, one thousand eight hundred metres at its summit, and the log cabin where Kim Jong-Il was born. Here are some extracts:

The story takes place in 1947. Dear Leader Kim Jong-Il was preparing noodles with his mother to feed the Head of State Father Great Leader. Dear Leader went away for a moment and returned with a pear in his hand. His mother had given it to him some hours previously. 'What, didn't you eat it?' his mother asked. 'No, I kept it for the Head of State Father Great Leader, to refresh him.' And the Dear Leader added: 'With cut pears crumbled on top, noodle soup tastes even better.' [*The words of Kim Jong-Il are accentuated in bold italics in the text, to stress their importance.*] 'Father's favourite dish has always been noodles' (in bold italics). And his father replied, 'But how do you know?' (in bold italics). 'Because mother told me, and it was the same at the battle of Paektosan, in which I also fought' (in bold italics).

Five children, including Dear Leader Kim Jong-Il, are playing with a miniature aeroplane, a cannon, a tank and an armoured train. 'Which is the most powerful?' asks one of the children. One replies, 'The aeroplane!' And the others, in sequence, the cannon, the tank and the armoured train. 'No!' Dear Leader Kim Jong-Il announces. 'It is the army that uses these weapons that is the most to be feared. Moral: man is stronger than all weapons, because it is he who made them and he who uses them.'

Kim Il-Sung is teaching Kim Jong-Il how to ski-jump. Kim Jong-Il falls the first time, but his father encourages him to start again. He starts again, and again he falls. His father tells him: 'That's enough for today!' But Kim Jong-Il, although his whole body is in pain, refuses, starts again and finally succeeds. Then he turns to his father and says to him, 'Skiing isn't difficult, what counts is willpower.' 'You are right,' his father replies with a look of pride.

In Lesson 8 we are told, with a straight face, that 'one plus one equals one'.

Dear Leader Kim Jong-Il is listening to a class in nursery school. The teacher says: 'One apple plus one apple equals two apples.' Dear Leader gets to his feet and protests: 'No, one plus one equals one!' He takes two pieces of plasticine and lumps them together in support of his thesis. He also gives the example of water which, when mixed together, still makes one. The other pupils then recognise the rightness of the Dear Leader's observation, and begin to exclaim, 'He's right, there's no doubt about it!' The teacher is left speechless and the pupils have learned a new thing thanks to Dear Leader Kim Jong-Il: one plus one does not always equal two.

This curious arithmetic was no doubt supposed to illustrate the imminent reunification of Korea under the leadership of Kim Jong-Il. But it was by no means the only instance in which politics inspired lessons. For example, I still resent my mathematics books, of which some extracts follow:

Some Young Pioneers are going to visit a historic site commemorating a battle led by the Great Leader. On the way there, they travel at 92 km/h and on the way back at 54 km/h. If we know that the journey there took three hours, how long will the return journey take?

On a collective field of 1.37 hectares, the harvest totals 1,294.65 tonnes. Before the liberation, only

219.2 tonnes were harvested on the same area. How many more tonnes have the farmers harvested after the liberation?

The people's army, after a battle against the armies of the American imperialist dogs and the South Korean puppets, took 15,130 soldiers prisoner. Among them were 1,130 more American bastards than South Korean puppets. How many American dogs and South Korean puppets were there?

The respected Great Leader Kim Il-Sung and the Dear Leader Kim Jong-Il had great consideration for children, and built a Palace of Children for them. Yong Chol lives three kilometres from the palace. To get there, he walks at a speed of 80 metres per minute. But after one kilometre he bumps into Chol Su and chats to him for five minutes. Bearing in mind that he had to be on time for his appointment, and that he has just lost five minutes, at what speed does he now have to walk to get there on time?

During the Korean War, 564 Chinese fighters and 45 Russian fighters joined forces with a unit of 789 fighters from the Popular Democratic

Republic of Korea to repel the invasion of the puppets of South Korea. How many fighters are there in all?

A little girl, a member of the Young Pioneers, is acting as a messenger to our patriotic troops during the war against the Japanese occupation. On a secret mission, she carries messages in a basket containing five apples, but is stopped by a Japanese soldier at a checkpoint. The wretched Japanese eats two of her apples. How many is she left with?

276 of Kim Il-Sung's soldiers are fighting against 577 Japanese. They kill 431. How many are left, and how many soldiers altogether are left on the battlefield, if we know that the losses among our ranks are three times less?

In Korean class, the texts that we read glorified our brave and heroic soldiers, like Isubo who, having lost both arms in a bombing raid, nonetheless continued firing his machine-gun by pressing on the trigger with his teeth. One of his companions, another hero, had deliberately allowed himself to be torn to shreds by enemy fire from a bunker so that his comrades could take an enemy position in the rear.

Other texts in our course books stigmatised the misdeeds of religion. I particularly remember one of them. The action took place in the forties. The text told the story of the theft of an apple from the orchard of a foreign missionary by a starving Korean child. The missionary caught the child and etched the word 'thief' on his forehead in acid!

More generally, our schoolbooks spent page after page glorifying the 'victory' of the PDRK* against Japan in 1945 and against the United States and the Southern puppets in 1953.† And just as the definitions in our dictionaries were politicised, we were trained to speak in ready-made phrases. We didn't say 'the Americans' but 'the American imperialists' or 'the American bastards' or even the '*yangkubegi*' (western long-noses). Rather than using the neutral term 'the South Korean government', we had to opt for 'the puppets of the South' or the '*keredodang*' (puppet bandits). For the Japanese, in the context of the war of liberation, we had to say 'the bastard Japanese'. For the South Korean presidents we were not to say 'President

---

* People's Democratic Republic of Korea, the official name of North Korea.
† In fact, North Korea was invaded by Russian troops and was not liberated by the armies of Kim Il-Sung. As for the Korean War (1950–3), it did not conclude with a victory of the North over the South, because the demarcation line was left unchanged at the end of the fighting.

Chun Doo-Hwan', but simply 'Chun Doo-Hwan', which sounds contemptuous.

From the beginning of secondary school we had classes in 'Communist morality'. I remember one chapter called 'Battle against the phenomena of transgressions against the law': 'Crimes are divided into two categories. Anti-revolutionary crimes and general crimes. An anti-revolutionary crime is an act against the state that attacks the security of the rights of a socialist country and the socialist system. For example, plotting to overthrow the socialist system, betrayal of the people and the fatherland, escape abroad, escape to the enemy side or giving support to the enemy. Anti-revolutionary crime has its roots in a hatred of the working class.'

We also spent a vast amount of time annotating the official ideology, *'juché'*, which can be translated as 'self-sufficiency' (in the sense of 'sufficient unto itself'). The *'juché* view of the world', our manuals said, 'is the most scientific and the most revolutionary view, for man is placed at the centre of everything'.

Duties

We had school from Monday to Saturday afternoon. After class, every day, we had to do agricultural work for two or three hours. On Sunday we laboured all day, with a picnic at lunchtime in the collective fields. In spring we planted seeds;

in August and September we harvested them. We also had to do the weeding. When the class went to the fields, the teachers lined us all up at the bottom of a hill, to attention, with our hoes over our shoulders. Then they made us climb to the top, hoeing the earth. Then we sowed. To get that duty out of the way as quickly as possible, we had races. There were hardly any adults around when we were working, and at times I got the impression that we children did most of the work in the fields.

The adults took charge of the ploughing. They sometimes used a tractor, but most of the time they used a wooden cart with an iron-tipped ploughshare, pulled by an ox or a cow. But at the start of spring, before the earth had been turned, it was the task of the schoolchildren to break the frozen ground so that the plough could pass through it. It was very demanding work. Some of us, myself included, tried to avoid those duties, even though they were compulsory in our little primary class. The first time I had to perform this burdensome task, at about the age of seven, has remained a lasting memory: the teachers had made us sing on the way from school to the fields, with a long hoe over our shoulders which we all had a great deal of difficulty carrying.

The pace of this labour stepped up from secondary school onwards: the whole class camped in the fields during the harvests, and there was no getting out of it. This terrible ordeal lasted a month and a half, during which all we did was work the earth until we were stiff all over. During the holidays, we grew maize, millet, rice, beans and rye. The teachers, who sometimes worked us to the point of exhaustion, were very hard on us. I would have to say that they were highly motivated, because the more work their class got through for the farmers, the greater their food bonus when it came to distribution. We, on the other hand, had no particular rights at all. So, in short, the harder we slaved, the more the teachers got to eat. The only 'bonus' we got lay in stealing ripe ears of maize here and there and hiding them in our shirts, grilling them on the sly afterwards. But it was better not to be caught pinching anything: if that happened, the teachers made us spend additional hours in the fields, until we were completely exhausted.

To encourage our work in the fields, the teachers made the first task planting the plots of land with pretty red and yellow pennants, the colours of the national flag. The hills were festooned with them, from the valleys to the peaks. Trailers pulled by little tractors, when there were any, or by an ox most of the time, were our shared transport. They too were decorated with red and yellow flags, a good omen for the harvests. As we hoed, sowed or harvested, we were subjected to a continuous flood of revolutionary songs, always very cheerful, broadcast by a propaganda lorry equipped with enormous loudspeakers. Although there are very few vehicles in Onsong, there were at least three propaganda lorries, which travelled the city and the surrounding villages. On top of that, in every district pylons fitted with loudspeakers broadcast Party orders and martial music that woke us every morning. So I always went to school to the sound of loudspeakers, and sometimes hummed the songs that I heard, which invariably mentioned the names of the Great Leader Kim Il-Sung and Dear Leader Kim Jong-Il. On holidays, the birthdays of the two Kims, New Year's Day, the Day of the Foundation of the Party, the Day of the Foundation of the Army, the Day of the Dead, Children's Day and 1 October, the loudspeakers in the village broadcast uninterruptedly throughout the day. There was also, of course, a PA system at the school, although it was used mostly during collective gymnastics.

The summer holidays lasted from early July to the end of August, while the winter holidays stretched from mid-November to March. But we didn't have much time to enjoy ourselves during these breaks because, apart from work in the fields, we had to do our homework in a group assigned to us. The composition of these groups, which were usually made up of four pupils, was decided by the teachers. Each of us went to one group or another, and each group had one pupil who had been appointed 'homework leader', because regardless of the activity there always had to be a designated leader. Our homework duties chiefly involved revising the subjects we had learned during the year, from maths to classes in the 'Era of childhood'. In the new term, we had to know these two books by heart, each of them eighty pages long. It really was tedious in the extreme, but fortunately our teacher helped us by guiding us towards the important passages that we had to learn at all costs. Our other holiday homework involved copying out endless pages. It was quantity that counted, and we saw to it that we did as much as possible. Generally, we tried to get all the copying finished by February, so that we had another month ahead of us to go skating on the frozen river.

Part of the 'homework' that we were given consisted of helping our parents around the house. But some of the other tasks were much more tiresome. Our teachers gave each of us collection quotas. We had to collect fifty bundles of maize leaves, which were then dispatched to paper factories. This meant that we spent whole days at a time unwrapping the ears of corn and tying up the bundles. There was also a quota of paper to be recycled, which we picked up all over the place, and quotas of copper and other metals that we had to find. We went all around the city and countryside dragging wooden handcarts from one place to another. We delivered our loads to a place set up

69

for the purpose within the school walls. Everything was counted by the teachers, who ticked boxes on a sheet every time we brought in a cart of paper, a few kilos of copper or bundles of maize skin. If we hadn't fulfilled our quotas by the time school started up again, we were awarded a bad mark, which counted for a great deal in our final school report.

During the winter holidays, there was also a dung quota to fulfil. To do this we had to carry six whole carts of faecal matter to the school, collected from public or private latrines. But we had to be careful not to choose just any old excrement. We needed human turds, the only ones that bore the label 'manure' in the eyes of our teachers. In extremis, dog turds were tolerated as well. But cowpats, horse manure and the liquid faeces of pigs or poultry were not acceptable. That said, we weren't averse to adding small quantities of forbidden excrement to bulk up our quotas because, scour the streets of the city though we did, dog poo was not easy to find, not least because adults collected it to fertilise their own private plots of land. Once I nearly came to blows with a neighbour over a piece of dog shit!

This prospecting work wasn't exactly a picnic. Since the temperature fell to minus twenty or thirty degrees in the winter, the human excrement was frozen. So we needed to use a pick or a hatchet to break up the piles of matter that spilled from the back of the rudimentary outdoor toilets by each dwelling. These wooden comfort stations were suspended over a deep hole dug in the ground, which sometimes extended into a kind of trench to the rear. This arrangement made our mission easier, because it meant that we only needed to prospect in the extension of that cesspit. Blows of the pick, blows of the shovel – we sometimes picked up pieces of matter as big as ourselves. This meant that a cart could be loaded up all at once, which came as a great relief to us, freezing, valiant Young Pioneers that we were.

Cesspits in the shape of a simple hole made our task more complicated. We had to lift the wooden plank overhanging the great ordure-filled opening, and slave away laboriously to cut into the conical pile that had accumulated over time.

We would then spread all of this malodorous material in the fields during the school year, beneath the vigilant eyes of the members of the brave teaching body. It was in this way that they sought to inculcate within us the courageous revolutionary virtues inspired by the glorious thoughts of Great Leader Kim Il-Sung and Dear Leader Kim Jong-Il.

Self-criticism

It was impossible to make fun of the two Kims in North Korea. No one would have dreamed of doing any such thing. It would have been suicide. I had never dared to let any such thought cross my mind. But once, stupidly, at the age of ten, I started drawing Kim Il-Sung, reproducing the badge I wore on my chest. The boy sitting next to me immediately reported me. He jumped to his feet, yelling in that monotonous voice that is sometimes used in the army: 'Teacher! Hyok is insulting our beloved Great Leader!' I immediately felt like a goldfish in a pond full of carnivorous perch. The teacher made me stand in the middle of the class and, for a good five minutes, thrashed me all over my body, giving me some of the hardest blows I have ever had in my life. She was bawling like a hysteric: 'How dare you draw our Great Leader! You little reactionary! That kind of thing will put you in front of a firing squad! Even a little squirt like you should understand that!' Then she made me stay on my knees at the back of the class for the rest of the day. I have never forgotten that lesson, not least because my teacher wanted to drag me to my parents' house to inform them of my unforgivable crime – a crime of which I myself was utterly convinced I was guilty. Fortunately, my long, loud sobs managed to soften her heart. She explained that only a few especially gifted draftsmen in North Korea had been authorised to reproduce portraits of the Great Leader. Anyone else impudent enough to want to depict Kim Il-Sung or his son deserved punishment.

'The Child Is the Future'

I finally got off with a lengthy session of self-criticism.
I was used to that kind of exercise in humility. Unless you
could get hold of one of the forms drawn up for the purpose, you had to take a clean white sheet with 'Letter of
Criticism' written at the top. Then you had to write as
best you could, to show that you were demonstrating a
'good attitude'. The content was always more or less the
same: 'At a particular date, at a particular time, during a
particular class, I became guilty of a particular thing . . .
The teacher reprimanded me harshly . . . But I was
unaware of the consequences of my actions . . . I am taking
the firm resolution never again,' etc. The longer the piece
of self-criticism, the better. Ten pages are better than five.
So you have to season your contrition with commentaries,
digressions, expressions filled with political jargon, useless
words, synonyms and all kinds of repetitions. Emphasis is
the most important ingredient in this bitter dish, in which
adverbs (basically . . . resolutely . . . truly . . . firmly) act as
a kind of sweetener. The self-criticism most easily digested
by the authorities has a certain pontificating tone: 'I am
going to work seriously to serve society and our fatherland, to become someone useful to our country, a servant
worthy of the trust of Generalissimo Comrade Great
Leader Kim Il-Sung.' And as the icing on the cake you
need a grandiloquent, solemn oath in which you declare
that you will never again blunder into such monumental

errors unworthy of a good socialist member of society. Then you add the date and sign.

We were all quite skilled at acts of contrition of this kind. Every Monday, in fact, we had to hand our teacher a form entitled 'The Whole of Daily Life', which we filled in more or less assiduously each Sunday. The form was divided horizontally into three parts. At the top, you had to draw up a list of the bad actions committed during the previous week, and repent for them in ready-made formulas. The box that followed was reserved for the good resolutions that you had taken since, and vows never to repeat the offence. The whole last part of the sheet was devoted to the denunciation of fellow pupils. Filling it in was compulsory, and everyone mutely complied. The teacher strongly advised us that if we were to get good marks, we should report at least two of our classmates, but some keen pupils cheerfully exceeded their quota. So every Monday the same ritual took place: each pupil had to read 'The Whole of Daily Life' out loud to the class. The pupils targeted by the denunciations had to rise to their feet, lower their heads, their chins pressing into their chests, and admit their mistakes, because you don't challenge your incrimination. So my drawing of Kim Il-Sung brought me the admonitions of thirty-five of my classmates. It was absolute hell, because each time it happened I had to stand up in class once again and tell the whole class how remorseful I was.

'The Child Is the Future'

These compulsory mutual denunciations often ended badly once school was over. Punches and kicks were exchanged. But the results of those small acts of revenge were, in turn, displayed to everyone the following Monday, gradually creating a climate of general suspicion. We couldn't be sure of anyone, so we all grew suspicious of each other, and that was precisely our teachers' aim.

However, we did reach certain accommodations with the rules. Under normal circumstances I, like my classmates, had very few 'bad actions' to confess to. But even so, I still had to come up with some to fill in Monday's form. This was also true of the section on compulsory sneaking. So we sometimes agreed among ourselves: 'You grass me up for calling a girl a specky weasel-face, and in return I'll rat on you for calling me a jerk . . .' Any pupils who got writer's block when they tried to fill in their forms often pounced on a denunciation read out by a classmate, and repeated it word for word themselves.

This ritual, into which we were initiated at the age of seven or eight, in the first year of primary school, taught us three cardinal values of adult life: the virtues of mutual suspicion, the tutelary benefits of lying and the advantages of bribes. For as we had discovered in primary school, these criticism–self-criticism sessions provided us with a wonderful means of exerting pressure on others, and an unparalleled means of threatening retaliation against a rival.

75

Conversely, a gift of a sweet or a cigarette was highly effect-ive in dissuading a powerful snitch from attacking you. All in all, the most cunning, the most underhand, the biggest mouths, not to mention the most affluent, almost always got the best deals. The most obsequious didn't do too badly either. In short, our class was a little microcosm of the social paradise for which our teachers were so selflessly preparing us.

Flowers for the leader

Every year on the birthdays of Kim Il-Sung and Kim Jong-Il, 15 April and 16 February respectively, everyone in our school had solemnly to climb the marble steps of Onsong hill leading to the giant statue of Kim Il-Sung, to deposit bunches of flowers. Each of us had to bring three flowers, of any colour but of a certain minimum size. They were usually peonies, and had to be bought from special green-houses reserved for ceremonial flowers, where gardeners did a thriving trade. They also sold *Kimilsungia*, a kind of pink orchid that serves as a horticultural reincarnation of Kim Il-Sung. His son also had his own floral avatar, a mag-nolia called *Kimjongilia*.

Those of us without enough money had an alternative plan. With my friends, Choljin, Kuanyok and Kuanjin, I jumped over the walls of a factory that grew the flowers that usually decorated the doorways to entrance halls, to chop some bouquets for ourselves. Sometimes we got caught by the guard, who would give us a good hiding. But most of the time we managed to get away, which meant that our floral booty was of excellent quality. And it was with great pride that we joined our class and stood in reverent contemplation of the products of our burgling expeditions, now draped around the bronze giant.

There were about three hundred of us, all in a row, walking in step in our school uniforms, washed by our mothers the day before. As we didn't have an iron, we put the uniform under the mattress to smooth it out. Ideally, you would have a crisp crease along your trouser leg. According to the rules, girls had their hair cut straight at ear height. Boys' hair was not to be more than a few millimetres long. All pupils wore the red scarf of the *Sunyondan*, the Young Pioneers, around their necks.

At the age of eight, in the second year of primary school, we started applying for membership of this organisation. As a rule, you joined the ranks of the Young Pioneers at about ten, and stayed there until the end of primary school. The best pupils in the class joined the movement on the day of Kim Jong-Il's birthday, the 16 February. The not-so-good pupils had to wait until the birthday of Kim Il-Sung, 15 April. And everyone else, the dregs, had to wait for Children's Day, the 6 June. These dates were usually decided by the teachers on the basis of everyone's marks. But in fact there was a fair amount of corruption in the air. Anyone could get a few strings pulled in exchange for the odd bottle of *soju* slipped to a teacher. During the ceremony of the awarding of the scarf, we had to swear an oath of allegiance to Kim Il-Sung and Kim Jong-Il. But that wasn't all. We also had to learn by heart a text about ten pages long, outlining the recent history of Korea. There were dozens and dozens of names of battles and the names of generals, with their dates of birth. What absolute torture! I remember it took a whole week of intense concentration, which ended up giving me a nose-bleed. We had to recite that endless screed before the whole class. The presentation lasted half an hour. The pupils' intonation varied according to their memory; the flood of words stopped, and then, after a bit of prompting from the teacher, started up again, even faster than before, then stopped again, and so on. The slower children spoke in bursts, like someone firing a machine-gun. The ones who couldn't get through all this verbiage were accepted anyway, but as a last resort, because everyone, without exception, had to become a Young Pioneer. And all Young Pioneers wore a badge on their chests, on the side of their heart. It bore the words 'Always Ready' in the colours of the national flag.

Corporal punishment awaited those of us who couldn't

get hold of a bouquet for the birthdays of the two Kims. This was also true if we hadn't done our homework. In this case our teachers would give us about ten blows of the cane, sometimes to the face, or punch us in the forehead and the stomach. We often had nosebleeds. But whatever happened, we had to try and stand upright, without a murmur, and take the blows as impassively as possible. We underwent these little tortures in front of the whole class. First of all the teacher read out a list of the pupils who were going to be punished, and the guilty parties had to line up facing them. We each tried to get to the back, to put off taking the blows for as long as possible. Then the teacher passed in front of us, walloping us hard. At the end of this civics lesson we had to clean the classroom, the corridor and the toilets. If the teacher was in a bad mood, he made us stay in silence in the corridor for a whole day, standing to attention or on our knees, or with our arms in the air like prisoners. From experience, I can tell you that the last of these positions is incredibly painful if you have to maintain it for more than an hour. Terrible punishments were also inflicted on pupils who had been absent from class. But if you had to draw up a scale for the severity of these corporal punishments, I would say that not bringing flowers to put at the foot of the statue of Kim Il-Sung was a more serious mistake than neglecting to do your homework.

On the birthdays of Kim Il-Sung and Kim Jong-Il, my classroom mission consisted of drawing and painting, over and over again, the birthplaces of our two illustrious rulers on large sheets of paper. Kim Il-Sung was born at the home of his grandmother in Mangyongde, and Kim Jong-Il in Changilbon, one of the peaks closest to Mount Paektu. I decorated my drawings, which were designed to be hung up in the classroom, with friezes of *Kimilsungia* and *Kimjongilia*. Rumour had it that Kim Jong-Il was actually born in the Soviet Union.* There was a song about an illustrious character born in Siberia, who was named only by his Russian first name. It was rumoured to be about Kim Jong-Il, and singing the song was forbidden. I was careful not to sing it. Not least because, as far as I was concerned, the official version was entirely dependable.

I proudly wore a badge of Kim Il-Sung and one of Kim Jong-Il. I swapped them around every few days, for no special reason. But we always had to wear one. For children, this was recommended from nursery school, although in primary school the badge of the Young Pioneers served just as well. But as soon as you entered secondary school, a badge of Kim Il-Sung or Kim Jong-Il on your heart

---

*Kim Jong-Il was in fact born in Russia, where he spent his childhood. He had adopted the Russian nickname of 'Yura'.

became entirely compulsory. You had to buy them, but they weren't expensive, apart from the very latest ones, which were generally more detailed in appearance. In the last series that I saw, the portraits were surrounded by a wreath of flowers. Some badges were circular, and others square with the flags of the Party and the country. They were all made of tin covered with a layer of gold paint.

I now realise that school had managed to inculcate such conformist behaviour in us that it became second nature. For example, when the teacher asked the pupils to choose one of their number to 'perform a particular mission', or to vote for the most meritorious among us, the class invariably selected the one that the teacher wanted to see promoted. Our choices always followed the established social hierarchy in every respect. Even if in theory we had complete freedom in our choice of candidate, each of us had a very clear idea of who had come from a more or less favoured family, and the children of Party worthies always wore leaders' stripes. They were also the ones to give the most money at the regular collections designed to finance 'good deeds', such as the decoration of the school on the birthdays of the two Kims. The teachers were often obsequiously polite to the children of the affluent: 'Hello, how are you? Is your mother well? I'd love to drop in and see her.' All that as a way of angling for an invitation to stuff their fat faces at the expense of the pupils' families. As the teachers were well in with these privileged little creatures, they indulged their whims while giving everyone else a sound thrashing.

Given that my family, being originally from Japan, was financially comfortable though politically vulnerable, the teachers didn't put themselves out on my behalf. In the middle of class, the teacher might say to me, knowing that my grandmother made them, 'I'd just love a little *yot* [caramel sweet]!' Which meant that I had to dash home and bring them some. The teacher would then cheerfully devour their *yot* in front of our class of anaemic and starving pupils. If I refused, he would glower at me for days, and the blows would come down as surely as the snow in winter. Once a teacher, Comrade An, learned that my father had just received a money order from Japan, and asked me to persuade my father to lend him some money. My father refused, saying that he couldn't do it without some kind of guarantee. After that, for the whole year I had a terrible time with this teacher, who was constantly losing his temper with me. When I failed to do my homework, I got double thrashings, and he was forever sending me to do his shopping. One time I had to tidy the classroom every day for three weeks, all on my own, when under normal circumstances four of us would have been doing the job! I should add that on that occasion I had skipped class for two days. With a friend of my age (I was eleven at the time), I had come across some crushed maize and beans, which we had fried up at my house when my parents were out. What a treat! We finished off our feast with some bread, spirits and cigarettes that we had swapped for a bag of maize. We drank *soju* and smoked as much as we could. What fun we had! The next day, we were so frightened of being taken to task that we skipped class again and made for the mountains. The day after, the teacher was resolutely waiting for us, his hands on his hips.

I hated all of my teachers. Their moods changed very quickly, like turkeys, suddenly flying into a rage for no reason at all. The worst punishment I ever had was at the hands of a female teacher: blows from the ruler on my body, punches to my face. I was nine, and she stopped when my nose started bleeding. But I eventually had my revenge. This horrible woman was a spinster, and therefore supposed to remain a virgin. But one night, by chance, I saw her holding the hand of a mechanic from the village . . . the very same guy who had owed my father money for years and refused to pay him back. My dad regularly went to his house and threatened to take his belongings, his television, some of his clothes and once even his motorcycle, so that he would finally pay his debt. Then, as though in passing, I mentioned that amorous encounter to my father, who practically went through the roof. He set off at a lick. After almost breaking down the mechanic's door, he gave him a good slap and yelled, 'So how did you get to screw your little teacher, eh? You know she's supposed to keep her virginity . . . So tell me, how did you manage to sweet-talk her?' What a sight, and how I laughed! The problem was that afterwards the same teacher gave me an even worse time than she had before. The rest of the year was a real ordeal.

On patrol

In groups of seven, we were assigned in turn to make nightly patrols of the school. In our minds, this mission placed a great responsibility on our shoulders, because we were supposed to give the alert if the American imperialists or a group of South Korean puppets suddenly landed to attack or spy on our establishment. Obviously there was nothing to spy on in our school, and of course nothing ever happened. But in spite of everything, we were always mobilised. Didn't the coat of arms of the Young Pioneers sewn on our uniform jackets say 'Always Prepared'? The patrols were a way of preparing us for military training. Rifle-shooting started in the third year of secondary school, at about the age of thirteen or fourteen. We were all very impatient to get started. The war, as we were constantly being told, could break out at any moment, and the 'highest level of vigilance' was required. It was, in fact, as though we were at permanent war, even though there was not the slightest actual conflict.

During these patrols we were armed with big truncheons studded with rusty nails, and a formidable weapon invented by a North Korean: the pepper grenade. This projectile consists of a blown hen's egg filled with red pepper, and protected by a little cotton net. If we had discovered a South Korean puppet or an American terrorist, he wouldn't have survived for long in the face of our fearless squad, always 'prepared to die to defend the Dear Leader, Kim Jong-Il'. Our prey would have been blinded by pepper grenades exploding on his body, and we would then have thrown ourselves on him, walloping him with our nailed truncheons. Nothing of the kind ever happened, and our arsenal was never used. But in my dreams, I saw myself repelling the enemy, defeating him, and then being hailed as a hero in Pyongyang by the Great Leader himself.

We had a lot of fun on these patrols. It was on one of them that I saw my first telephone. No one uses them in North Korea, apart from cadres and the military. Two of them, without dials, were clearly visible in the staff room and the sentry box by the entrance. At first we had no idea how they worked. But we finally got the hang of it. You picked up the receiver, an operator came on the line, and you told him, in a loud voice, 'Hello, I am the General

Secretary of the Party, I'd like to speak to Mr Kim . . .', and then you hung up, bursting with laughter.

By the age of ten or twelve, we weren't averse to smoking cigarettes and drinking *soju* while on patrol. Normally, we were supposed to stay awake all night. But as we were often drunk, none of us ever spent a sleepless night exactly. We ended up going to sleep in the school sentry's little cabin. The girls had a special room to themselves to rest in, but they couldn't escape either our sarcasm or our liking for jokes. Many times we surprised them when they were fast asleep, disguised as thieves to frighten the life out of them. Some of us were happy to go on patrol to get close to the girls that we happened to fancy. But the girls armed themselves with hardened apricots, and the intruder would immediately be repelled by a storm of projectiles.

My three best friends, Choljin, Kuanyok and Kuanjin, and I became inseparable from secondary school onwards. Our friendship lasted until I left for China. We smoked cigarettes, we drank spirits, we stole from the fields. We pinched crushed maize from our neighbours' kitchens, then swapped it for buns that we hid at the bottom of our satchels. We shared everything. If one of us managed to get his hands on a quantity of food, he immediately shared it with the others.

Our favourite reading was a propaganda comic devoted to daily life in South Korea. It was while reading and re-reading this that I began to develop a taste for drawing. It was called *The Rotten World is Sick*. Thanks to this comic, which came stamped with the Party seal, we learned that children in South Korea were too poor to go to school, and that they had to work from early childhood. We learned that gangs of boys polished shoes and sold cigarettes to survive. Many of them were starving to death. At the same time, some South Koreans were giving jewels to their dogs. In the capitalist Korea described to us in this comic, everyone was at risk of being murdered on the next street corner, fires broke out daily, the countryside was swarming with bandits, there were dozens of burglaries every day, road traffic was complete anarchy and there were accidents all over the place.

Inspired by a passion for drawing, we had assembled a collection of our own best work. We tended to imitate the style of *The Rotten World is Sick*, trying to be even more damning. Food was our main preoccupation; for example, we had imagined a grotesque competition being held in the United States, where the winner was the one who ate the most. We had drawn several pages on this subject, which struck us as completely unlikely. What we didn't know at the time was such competitions really did exist in the western world.

4

'Let Us Not Live for Today, Let Us Live Today for Tomorrow'

Wormwood and dandelions

In our district, there was a madman who sometimes went around without his trousers on, his crotch exposed. His name was Konzhangan, and he didn't wear the badge of Kim Il-Sung. His clothes were in rags, and he was constantly scratching the lice from his head. Everyone always laughed at him, even though he was in his fifties. He was one of the first victims of the famine. He got thinner and thinner and thinner, and then he was found one winter day with his nose in the snow.

The landscape changed a lot as famine and misery increased. The shortage of electricity meant that the pumps in the mines had to be switched off, and the mines filled up with water. As coal was now almost impossible to get hold of, people dashed to the mountainsides to cut wood. Within a few years, the hillsides had turned completely yellow, stripped of their vegetation. Then the rain that streamed down the denuded slopes took whole sections of land with it. Our mountain was unrecognisable.

There was no more rice, no more potatoes, even in small quantities. We moved on to noodles made of maize flour. The ear, the stem, the bulb, the leaves: everything was ground up in the factory to make this very special kind of pasta. But we were given the noodles in very small quantities, so we boiled them up in lots of water and served them in soup. You had to watch your teeth when eating them, because they had little stones inside. In everything they produced for the collective, the farmers had got used to slipping in incredible quantities of stone to keep to the quotas, which were measured by weight.

Later, our village started feeding itself on weeds like wormwood and dandelion. Sometimes people managed to make soup out of maize powder, but it had become very rare, in fact priceless, almost impossible to get hold of. Then we moved on to really vile food substitutes. Weeds, of whatever kind, were boiled up and swallowed in the form of soup. We picked these inedible leaves on the edges of the fields or the banks of the river. The soup was so bitter that we could barely keep it down, and the first and sometimes the second brew had to be thrown away. Only the third would be kept. Sometimes we used a machine to grind up the bags of grass that we collected.

In about 1994, my father started selling the electronic appliances that our family had brought us as gifts from Japan. Our stereo, our tape recorder and our television were bartered for maize flour from the cadres of the collective farms. Then, like everyone else, we started eating noodle soup, which my mother boiled for a very long time, making a very clear broth so as not to be wasteful. As we weren't consuming very much nourishment, we ate it in large quantities and ended up with hugely distended stomachs. The people of Onsong sold everything they possessed for food: tables, chairs, wardrobes, even their pots and pans. As some of our neighbours owed us money that they couldn't pay back, my father would drop in on them unexpectedly to demand a meal, or failing that he took away things that he would immediately sell. If we were lucky he got a chicken or a pig. Dad was a bit menacing, so the neighbours let him get away with it.

Everyone learned to live from one day to the next. The least well-off took up position along the road to the open market and called out to the farmers on their way to sell the little flour or food that they possessed, to see if they would sell their merchandise at a slightly lower price. Then they themselves went to the markets, or waited until evening when the prices of the goods went up. They made tiny profits of ten to twenty wons, enough for a bowl of noodles. My mother, who baked five-won buns, sometimes sold her goods for four wons fifty to intermediaries, which meant that she didn't have to spend the day at the market. At this time, in 1996, a kilo of maize flour cost fifty wons. A lot of swindling went on. One seller managed to sell some packs of American cigarettes to a cadre who, when he opened them up, discovered rolled-up paper instead of tobacco. Some sellers of chilli powder substituted coloured sawdust, others put nails in mushrooms to bulk up the weight.

Like many of the adults, I had to take up illegal work in the mine. I went there after school. The lignite that I dug from the walls with a little pick I sold on to buy food, or bartered it directly for maize. Need is a tyrant, and hundreds of adults and children did the same. Then the floods made this task difficult, dangerous, even impossible. There were lots of accidents due to collapses. Some foolhardy people neglected to support their improvised galleries and ended up buried alive when there were rock falls. From the winter of 1997, people dug hundreds of 'private' holes, despite the fact that this was forbidden. The holes were big square orifices that opened straight down into the fields, and

91

extended by horizontal gullies designed to join up with the State mine. There were so many of them that the fields threatened to collapse when the thaw came.

Behind our house, there was a little vegetable garden where we grew garlic and leeks. The perimeter was punctuated by bean plants. From 1995, we put barbed wire on the top of our wooden fence to keep our neighbours from stealing from us. But that didn't really dissuade the starving people, and we had kilos and kilos of beans pinched. People like my grandmother, who raised pigs, started to erect electrified fences around their pigsties. But with increasingly frequent electricity cuts they weren't really that much use. Finally, following the example of many pig-breeders, they ended up keeping their inestimable curly-tailed future food source in the house with them. In this way many houses were turned into pigsties, although even that didn't always deter thieves.

In 1996, we were the victims of an attempted break-in. At the time I was living in the big house of my paternal grandparents along with my mother and father. We had barricaded ourselves in for the night when we heard sounds of fighting coming from outside: one of our cousins who lived not far away had surprised three soldiers who were trying to enter one of the unoccupied rooms of the house by forcing a window. Dashing outside, we found my cousin half-unconscious. He had been beaten with sticks; the soldiers were making off towards a little bridge that led to an army blockhouse. At least we knew who the guilty parties were. The next day, my father went to negotiate with them, and although they continued to deny their involvement, the soldiers gave us a hundred kilos of maize. My dad has a lot of nerve, and knows how to get respect!

Some of these starving soldiers formed gangs to loot houses and steal chickens and other domestic animals. They worked at night. People were so frightened of them that the soldiers didn't even have to get their weapons out. Being highly esteemed in North Korea, they had a kind of immunity, and it wasn't hard for them to abuse their status. At first they only attacked private properties, little plots of land, individual supplies or family farmyards. But later they moved on to animals: pigs and even cattle.

In 1996 the government decided to have the army guard the fields against looting by the starving population. The plan was one of deterrence. A sentry box holding three soldiers was set up at each corner of the collective fields. There were also patrols day and night. The soldiers, it goes without saying, were happy to exploit the situation. These conscripts gladly accepted bribes – bottles of *soju*, pieces of bread, money – and then turned a blind eye to thefts. But it was very dangerous to venture into the fields without their say-so, since they had orders to shoot on sight. Justifying the adoption of such draconian measures, Kim

This Is Paradise!

Jong-Il had declared that any marauders stealing the property of the people 'would be treated like wild boar' – which amounted to saying that they deserved to be shot. This warning was posted up on all the walls of Onsong. In spite of everything, some desperate people dared to venture up to the edges of the fields of maize or courgettes to pinch a few corn cobs or vegetables which they ate discreetly as they walked. They were careful not to carry on their persons anything that might have compromised them. The soldiers systematically searched people who crossed a plantation, and anyone caught thieving ran the risk of execution.

In these hungry times, being put on field-guard duty was a very enviable situation for a soldier doing his military service. It was a sort of guarantee of survival, so that sinecure was reserved for the eldest, the ones who had already served at least half of their time in the army, more than six and a half years. The young conscripts were barely fed in the barracks, and enjoyed none of the advantages of their older colleagues. Their superiors, who carried out raids and food-thefts at night, forbade these private soldiers to go out at nightfall, to ensure that there weren't too many incidents, and to keep a monopoly on organised plunder. One of my cousins, who was in his first year of military service at that point, died of hunger in his barracks within just a few months because the older conscripts kept the small amount of food available all to themselves. Many of these young recruits, distinguished from the older conscripts by their bony frames, died of hunger in 1996 and 1997. Some of them were so weak that they couldn't even carry their rifles, which they sometimes dragged along behind them. The well-nourished fugitives coming back from China didn't have too much difficulty strangling these wretched squaddies if they were caught by them at the border. Everywhere in North Korea, wherever you looked, it was every man for himself, in the garrisons just as much as elsewhere.

By this point prices had gone through the roof. The price of a bottle of spirits had risen within a short space of time from ten to forty wons, while my father's salary was still one hundred and ten wons a month. It was then that my mother started selling buns and pancakes in the market. One day, an old man with very dirty hands made off with some of mum's buns, but she didn't have the heart to go after him. The dirty buns would have been spoiled in any case. There were also always starving children pinching things from the displays and running away. My mother was shattered by the sight of dozens of ragged urchins (some of them little more than toddlers) avidly watching the customers as they ate their pancakes just in case they accidentally dropped some. Then they would dart forwards to pick scraps up and stuff them into their mouths like birds pecking at crumbs. You could see them standing in wait by each food stall. The smallest and weakest of them knew very well that if they pinched a doughnut or a hand-ful of noodles from an adult's bowl, they would almost immediately be caught by the vigilant customer, who would kick them soundly. But they were so desperate that they still made off with any food that they could get their hands on, and without even taking the trouble to run away, so they could eat as much as possible immediately, even as they endured the often terrible blows of their victims. And some adults, racked with hunger, ruthlessly beat up and stole from children who were better off than they were. It was a world of anxiety, suspicion and fear, from which charity was absent.

Only agricultural products were authorised for sale in the private markets. For any others, dealers needed a licence from the State and had to pay a tax. But by 1997 or thereabouts, it was almost impossible to find a product manufactured in North Korea, as almost all the factories had come to a standstill. The only clothes we could buy came from China. So there was soon a certain tolerance for commerce in manufactured products: you only had to slip the inspectors a few cigarettes for them to turn a blind eye. Some Chinese street peddlers came to sell their products themselves, usually bartering them for seafood.

These Chinese tradesmen attracted so much envy that some of them were robbed, or even stabbed or stoned to death by starving people who lured them into sidestreets.

Although any kind of commercial dealings outside of the State circuits was forbidden, life was so hard that everyone traded more and more on the black market. My father, a resourceful man, had gone into the illicit seafood trade. He went to fish clandestinely on the coast, and sold his catch to Chinese traders in Onsong. He also made a remedy that was highly prized in China: frog oil. The precious liquid is found in tiny quantities in one of the amphibian's glands, and the creature has to be eviscerated in order to extract it. It takes hundreds of frogs to obtain a litre of the yellowish extract, which is secreted by the creatures just before they hibernate. He had to catch them in October, just before the frosty season, in Ongjin, in the southern region of Hwangyedo, and carry them back on his shoulders, walking at night to avoid checkpoints. Wires were slipped through the heads of the amphibians, and they were carried like a kind of necklace. There were big frog-breeding plants in Ongjin, and many people with a little money set aside invested it in the trade. Down in Ongjin, a frog cost nine wons, compared to fifteen wons in the north. But a kilo of frog oil could be sold for twenty thousand wons to Chinese traders! The attic of our house was sometimes full of bags of dead but not yet desiccated frogs. My father spent a lot of time removing the little glands, far from the eyes of our neighbours. The eggs were sold separately, as were the legs. The rest we ate. In order to survive, my father also got involved in smuggling Korean antiques to China, via a cousin of his. If he had been caught he could have been executed. Some antique smugglers were actually shot in Onsong.

Rumbling stomachs and the UN

My father was always telling me that it was important to be well dressed, to strike a fine figure and look well fed, even if you were dying of hunger. It was important not to attract contempt. In North Korea, other people's contempt is the worst insult of all. This philosophy of concealment was also one of power, because the most important thing of all was to conceal the poverty and distress of the populace from other countries.

Shortly after the start of the famine, international food aid destined for the nursery schools and kindergartens of Onsong began to arrive. For a while, a few months, I think, everyone was able to take advantage of it. There was rice in the dining-hall, and all the children started to get their strength back. But then the cadres decided to reduce the rations. First the children had to make do with soup, then with nothing. Once again they were so weak that they couldn't walk to school, and once again the building became completely deserted. The children spent their days in bed. Their faces were terribly thin, their cheeks were hollow and their eyes bulged with hunger.

The UN must have heard that the aid was not being distributed, because an inspection was organised in January 1998.* The Party cadres, who had been alerted in advance, had rice delivered to the dining-halls of the kindergartens and nursery schools. This rice came from the city storehouses, which were apparently far from empty. The whole Party hierarchy was very worried by this inspection, and official vehicles were soon scurrying around the city. The children and workers in the nursery schools were told that they would soon be able to enjoy a good meal, but that they would have to put the UN inspectors off the scent by telling them that this diet was perfectly normal. On the day of the visit there were all kinds of dishes on the menu: noodles, maize soufflé . . . The children that the UN officials spoke to had learned their lesson well and all declared that they always ate their fill. The only incident, which the

---

*In theory, the United Nations, via the World Food Programme (WFP), feeds six million North Koreans, or a third of the population.

inspectors apparently failed to notice, was the 'spontaneous' declaration of a kindergarten teacher, who said she wished the inspectors 'could come every day'. No doubt the foreigners thought this was merely politeness on her part.

The atmosphere changed completely once the UN team set off again. The cadres took back all of the food stored in the dining-hall kitchens, even removing uneaten food from the tables where the children were still sitting. I later learned that on the way back the UN inspectors had asked to pay unexpected visits to families, pointing at random houses. The cadres were quite used to this kind of exercise. Each time a request was made about a house whose inhabitants they knew to be undernourished, they insisted there was no one at home. But they did allow the foreigners to ask questions of the better-off families, who were almost always, and for good reason, Party leaders.

Everyone in Onsong was aware of these inspections, which had already taken place in neighbouring districts. It was always the same scenario, and no one was surprised to see things being played out exactly the same in our city. After the episode involving the UN inspection, no other international aid ever reached the inhabitants who were truly in need – apart from New Year's Day 1998, when some of the mine workers received a consignment that kept them in supplies for a fortnight or so. This was a delivery of maize flour for animal consumption, in sacks marked 'USA'.

The school of hunger

In our house, at first, we managed a little better than everyone else, thanks to the money sent to us some years previously by one of my great-uncles who had stayed in Japan. My mother tried to make this nest egg go as far as she could, spending it very parsimoniously. I usually ate two 'meals' a day, by which I mean clear soups with a few leaves of vegetables and some maize noodles. Now and again I was allowed some tofu. But it couldn't last.

As a harbinger of what was to come, when I looked out of our windows I could see people, our neighbours, most of them well dressed, collecting grass and tree bark – usually pine, or various shrubs – from the mountainside facing us. To get it into a form that was stomachable, they grated the bark and boiled it up before eating it. And much good it did them: their faces swelled from day to day until they finally perished.

When the son of one of our neighbours died, his body looked like a bag of bones. His parents, who had sold everything for food, didn't have a coffin or a shroud to bury him in, nor even a cart to carry his inert body to the mountain, so they borrowed ours. They wrapped the corpse in straw, carried it off and buried it as it was. The dead boy's mother died in the same circumstances two months later. She never complained, she didn't beg, until one day she came to beg my mother to give her, 'for one last time', some tofu soup. My mother couldn't refuse. She knew the woman was close to the 'yellow springs'.* She passed away the same day.

At school, the secondary teachers collectively cultivated a field of maize and beans adjacent to the school building. The primary teachers had to make do with flowerbeds around the buildings. It was very easy for the pupils to help themselves, and I was quick to do so. Sometimes I left school with two corn cobs in my pocket, and ate them when I got home. In about 1995, the teachers turned both flowerbeds and a field into a vegetable garden. They made the pupils dig and plant them. It goes without saying that everything was swiftly looted, because we were all hungry. The teachers tried their best to set up a guard system, but when we were assigned to protect the vegetable patches, we helped ourselves without their knowledge. In a situation like that, the more guards there were, the more thieves there were!

Everything was falling apart and wasting away around me. Slowly but surely, like a mud flow swallowing up the

---

* The land of the dead in oriental cosmogony.

mountain, hunger engulfed my little universe. And yet the pupils still had to go to school since it remained compulsory. The poorest lived on nothing but grass, and during class their stomachs rumbled. After a few weeks their faces began to swell, making them look well nourished. Then their faces went on growing until they looked as though they had been inflated. Their cheeks were so puffy that their view was impeded, and they couldn't see the blackboard. Some of them were covered with impetigo and flaking skin.

As time passed, there were fewer and fewer of us sitting at the school desks. Sometimes there were only about ten in a class of thirty-five. The poorest, who had nothing to eat at all, skipped school to go to the market, because at least there they could try and steal something to eat. The teachers, who were by now equally unable to cope, regularly announced a week or two of holidays, without explanation. Work in the fields was still compulsory despite the fact that both the remaining pupils and the teachers were extremely weak. We actually went there not to work, but to glean anything we could find to keep from starving to death.

In the end, just before I escaped in 1998, there were only eight or nine of us in class. The rest were too weak even to walk. Many of them fell sick with what the hospital doctor called 'general weakness'. There were three degrees of 'general weakness'. If you were diagnosed as 'third degree', it meant that you were at death's door.

The number of pupils at both primary and secondary school had dropped from one thousand five hundred to six hundred in the space of a year. My classmates started dying during the summer of 1996. Though these deaths were a result of the famine, they were also down to the fact that many parents left their homes in search of food, and most of them didn't come back. No doubt some of these adults starved to death themselves, while others probably ended their days in the penal labour colonies where they were interned after being caught stealing food. Finding themselves left to their own devices, children abandoned by their families at first said nothing, and acted as though everything was fine. Then they wasted away, ended up in the street or took to begging. In almost every case, they breathed their last just a few months later. In my class alone, four of my classmates were abandoned like this.

The children of the less favoured families deserted the school and were the first to die. But some of them managed to survive. These were the most resourceful, the smartest. They subsisted by scraping together leftovers, however small, pinches of rice grains, wheat or other cereals, in the market or along the railway tracks. But towards the end even they ran out of strength. You would see them constantly nodding off in class. It was a pathetic sight, and the teachers themselves no longer had enough energy to take their classes. They sat shapelessly in their chairs, cane in hand, while we repeated by heart lessons we had already learned about the childhoods of Kim Il-Sung and Kim Jong-Il.

In my class, when I moved to secondary school, four of my classmates died of hunger. Two girls and two boys. One of the two boys was called Kang Jin. His elder brother, who had done everything he could to help him, also died shortly afterwards. His name was Chang Song-Ho, and he had a slight mental handicap. I don't know what happened to him, but he stopped coming to school, and a few days later we learned that he had perished at home. One of the two girls was a very close friend. Her name was Ungyang. She was an orphan and lived on her own with her grandmother. One day she was so hungry that she started eating wild apricot stones. She stuffed herself with them and died of it. I went along to her house with some children from my class when we learned of her death. When I went in, her grandmother was weeping by her lifeless body. We had all clubbed together to give her grandmother some corn cobs. They were supposed to pay for Ungyang's funeral. It was a gift that later struck us as pretty derisory. I can't recall the other girl's name, I just remember her bandy legs. Her mother had already died of hunger and all she had left was her father and her little brother, who was himself on the brink of death. She had spent her days by her brother's bedside, going short herself so that he would have more to eat. Finally she died before he did. Without a doubt, many of the children in the class who had managed to survive until then were so weak that they didn't have very long to live themselves.

After we had stopped going to school we lost touch with one another, and I don't know what happened to most of the pupils. A few exceptions aside, there was little mutual aid among classmates, or neighbours. Each of us already had quite enough trouble looking after ourselves.

But I really didn't want to dissociate myself from Choljin, Kuanyok and Kuanjin. I went on frog hunts with them in the cornfields and paddy fields. We had barbecues of frogs' legs. What a feast! At sowing time, the children rushed into the fields to scoop out the grains that had just been put in the earth. We boiled them up and made gruel from them. But the hungriest children ate them raw, like birds. It was important not to be caught, so we usually went there at night. Obviously, by harvest-time, hardly anything was growing in the fields that we had targeted. We also plundered the potato and maize fields. These were easier to loot, because once the gang of children had entered the field, the height of the plants meant that the sentries keeping watch couldn't see us. If one of them happened to pass by, the child on guard duty alerted us with a whistle and we made off in all directions. We also tried to catch chickens from the collective chicken farms. My first experience of this was not a great success. I certainly managed to catch one along with a friend, but we were in such a hurry to kill it to fill our empty stomachs that I cut off a finger with my knife, thinking I was cutting the chicken's neck.

One day we found a little socialist paradise: a vast orchard full of watermelons, apples, pears . . . The place was hidden behind four rows of hills more than an hour's walk and climb away. A group of us went there at night. We set off at dusk to avoid arousing suspicions. A real expedition, we prepared sacks, a torch, knives . . . Once we were there, one of us went on sentry duty while the others caught and picked as much fruit as we could. Our sacks were enormous, and we could hardly drag them behind us. But hunger is stronger than anything. Even the runts, exhaustedly trailing sacks bigger than themselves, somehow managed to get all the way back along the paths, using the moonlight as a guide.

Sometimes we met adults who had given the guards bottles of spirits in exchange for a few sacks of fruit. By now we had learned that this was a collective farm whose products were reserved for export in the form of preserves. This made our incursions even more dangerous.

We could have been accused of 'sabotage of the country's foreign economic policy'. After a few months, the guards of this extraordinary orchard got wind of what we were up to, and one night we were surprised to discover that they had brought in three or four guard dogs. Some of us, myself included, were bitten to the bone, and we had to become extremely careful. My greatest fear was that I would catch rabies, because it is a common illness in North Korea. Tradition said that if we couldn't eat dog to avoid catching rabies, we could burn a tuft of dog hair and apply it to the bite.

Scapegoats

Every family in Onsong tried to scrape together a little more land to grow the vegetables that would allow them to survive. The cadres, although they lived in big houses with adjoining land, often reached some kind of an agreement with the department in charge of sharing out land to find unoccupied plots on the mountainside. As for ordinary people, they settled for the riverbanks, but since the slightest flood risked wiping out the fruit of their labours, they had to be constantly on their guard.

Apart from the cadres, there were other well-off people in the city, though they were the few privileged people of the regime who had gone abroad, to study, or who traded with

China. A saying distinguished three categories of rich people: *ganbu*, *kwabu* and *aobu* – Party cadres, fishermen and widows. The fishermen could always keep a little fish aside for themselves and sell it to make a little extra; widows are free women, in all senses of the term, and some of them prostituted themselves for money or food.

The famine unleashed a political purge. Many cadres whose loyalty was doubted by the regime, like the mayor of Onsong, were sent to 'take part in the revolution', a euphemism which meant dismissal followed by 're-education through work' in a manual job. The Minister of Agriculture, Kim Se-Kwan, was shot on the orders of Kim Jong-Il, on the pretext that he had sold seed to the United States. Disgrace in North Korea is almost always collective, and the purges were not confined to the incriminated cadre, or even to the limited circle of his immediate family and his colleagues: according to the rules, the purge affects three generations. In Onsong 'leader number eight', the cadre charged with sending the best agricultural products to the high cadres in Pyongyang, was related to the Minister of Agriculture who had just been sentenced. One night, in 1996 or 1997, I can't remember which, the security agents came to his house to get him, along with his wife and children. They were taken to a penal labour colony reserved for political prisoners, and no one ever heard of them again. It was one of that cadre's neighbours who whispered this terrifying story into the ear of my father, who passed it on to me much later, when we were in China. At the time, my father added, many people realised that these victims were merely scapegoats, because the regime had to justify the mistakes that had led to the famine.

Nocturnal disappearances had become very common in Onsong after 1995. I even noticed this myself. Everyone talked about it and trembled with fear as they conjured up the fate reserved for those unfortunate people. Everyone was aware that they too could disappear if they made a false move, or if a distant relative (some far-off cousin, for example) had fallen into disgrace. The camps had also filled with people who had gone to work illegally in China in order to buy food, and were caught on their return. Most of them were people who lived in border regions, as we did ourselves. Renegades were routinely sentenced to several months or even several years of camp. And things were even worse when the illegal worker was caught, on his way back, with one or more bibles. In China, dozens of Protestant South Korean missionaries distributed them for free, and many people, once converted, were tempted to bring them back. However, in North Korea the possession of a bible is considered a crime that deserves the death penalty.

My father also knew a smuggler who travelled back and forth between Korea and northern China. One day his step-mother, who had come to do his housework, discovered a bible hidden behind a cupboard. As she flicked through the 'good book', a neighbour assigned by the security services to check the political rectitude of the neighbourhood happened to drop by. She made off with the forbidden book, which she duly passed on to the local security office. In the mean-time, the smuggler had been alerted, and knowing that the game was up he decided to go into hiding and prepare for one last journey to China. He had no choice now: it was camp or exile. A month later, when his planned escape was all ready, he took the risk of going home at night to pick up his things. Security officers were waiting for him, and he was sent to a penal labour colony, never to be seen again. From what people said, renegades who were caught on their return from China were interrogated very intensely by the police for three months. They had to write down dozens of times the whole story of their offences and what they had done on the other side of the border. Through these police methods, the security agents always ended up discovering whether the renegade had had contact with Protestant pastors.

Scapegoats were needed everywhere and at every level, so that people could offload their anger on to them rather than on to the regime. Then, every two or three years, Pyongyang sent *groupa* – teams of investigators whose work consisted of digging out 'anti-socialist elements' – all around the country, sector by sector. It happened where we lived in 1996. A *groupa* consisting of twenty officials landed on us. As people were envious of us, despite our situation, my father's unit leader had his eye on us, and he had asked the investigators to check us first. He had accused us of hiding Japanese money in our house, which was true. Our Japanese family had actually left us some, as I have mentioned. But it was illegal. By law, we should have changed our Japanese yens into North Korean wons at the official exchange rate, but my father had refused to do this because the rate was poor. We were also accused of changing money on the black market. As our family had a reputation for being well-off because of our Japanese origins, Chinese traders came to us to change their Chinese yuans for Korean wons on the black market. This was known round about, and the unit leader accused my father of having considerable sums of money, which was dangerous, because you could find yourself accused of 'capitalism'.

But it was my mother who was called in by the *groupa*, who doubtless thought her more likely to make a confession. How wrong they were! The police questioned my mother about the use we had made of the money sent to us by our Japanese family. Had we changed it at the official rate, as the law said we must, or had we kept it? My mother assured him that we had acted perfectly legally. Then they asked her to list the purchases that we had made with our nest egg. Then, while she was about it, she had to repeat the list, then repeat it again. Seven times in all. Of course we still had some money, but my mother assured the security officers that it had all been spent. If she had said the opposite they would have confiscated everything we still had on the pretext of 'anti-socialist activity'. Seven times, then, my mother lied, drawing up a fictitious list of her expenditure. And she did so successfully, because the team finally let her go.

There were also teams of 'hunters' of anti-socialist elements at a local level, who were attached to the army. They could intervene at any time to 'counter the phenomenon of embourgeoisement and the accumulation of capital', of which people who practised private trade were held to be guilty. But their investigations were less intense than those of the special teams sent from Pyongyang on the orders of Kim Jong-Il, like the one we had just had to deal with. Such teams were primarily interested in the trade of luxury products with Chinese business partners, such as rare seafood, medicinal products, precious mushrooms or frog oil, because some people went to catch seafood, or bought it from fishermen, and then sold it on at a good price to Chinese traders. This trade was risky, and it required a lot of preparation. To reach the coastal zones, you had to get hold of a *yoheng zheng* (travel permit) from the army. You had to grease the palms of the soldiers, even if you had a plausible pretext (the funeral of a parent, a wedding . . .). The procedure took a week. Because we were in the middle of the famine, the few trains were jam-packed, and it became harder and harder for the authorities to check everyone's papers, so the number of fare-dodgers was constantly on the rise. If a check occurred, the fare-dodgers were well advised to have a bottle of spirits or a few packs of cigarettes ready to give to the policemen. Otherwise, the traffickers were sent to the *rodong danryeondae* (camp for re-education by labour) for several months.

It was even harder to go to Pyongyang without a permit, where all the most privileged people of the State and all the best social categories lived. It was impossible to obtain a travel permit for the capital without the 'invitation' of a member of your family living in Pyongyang. They would have to buy a numbered and certified document from the security officers, of which a stub would be sent to the local travel permit office ('office number two'), from which the person wishing to travel to the capital would have to go and collect it. When the train arrived in Pyongyang, the policemen checked the platforms against lists of names to see if they matched numbers on the stubs. If they didn't, the rail cheats would have to take the train in the opposite direction. Nonetheless, there were opportunities for them to escape the penal labour colonies, since they were in remote rural regions. Because of the shortage of fuel and transport, even the police weren't able to get them there.

The procedure was just as long and drawn out for North Koreans who wanted to go to zones close to the Chinese border, because most of the people who wanted to take that journey had only one thought in their heads: to flee to China to get away from the food shortages.

As I have said, the Party cadres always spoke in terms of 'natural disasters' when it came to explaining the reasons for the famine. They said it had rained too much and that the floods had wrought havoc through the whole of the country. In Onsong, apart from a few landslides, this wasn't really the case, but I thought that elsewhere in North Korea nature must have been much less kind. Anyway, since it was practically impossible to travel across the country, no one could verify this. The authorities also told us that the United States and South Korea bore some responsibility for the shortages, because it was they who had started the Korean War. According to the authorities, without that war Korea would have been reunified and none of this would ever have happened. So it was all the fault of the American imperialists and the Southern puppets. I completely accepted this reasoning, without asking any difficult questions. It was only many years later, once I had reached South Korea, that I discovered to my great confusion that the Korean War had been started not by the 'Southern puppets' but by Kim Il-Sung himself!

At around this time, television broadcasts showed propaganda films about countries that had abandoned socialism, such as East Germany and China. We were told that at first, in the states that had betrayed Marxism, everything had seemed rosy; then gradually the people became impoverished, were thrown into the street and ended up in misery. The commentator assured us that communism was the only possible future, and that consequently we must not leave North Korea; that there was no question of depending on other countries for trade or exchange, because that road led straight to national bankruptcy. That the precepts of 'self-sufficiency' contained in the philosophy of *juché* must be followed without fail. The population must remain staunchly loyal to Kim Il-Sung and Kim Jong-Il, now more than ever.

The official slogans changed as the famine ravaged the country. At the very beginning, in 1995, the cadres encouraged us to accept what was called a 'forced march towards victory'. The term referred to the 'forced march' undertaken by Kim Il-Sung and his partisans during the war against the Japanese occupying forces. The following year, the battle-cry was 'Let us speed up the forced march towards the final victory.' When hunger had reached its worst, another new slogan appeared: 'Let us not live today for today, but let us live today for tomorrow'. By now, the poorest people had been reduced to eating boiled pepper leaves or bean leaves. Some families came to beg us for left-over tofu that my mother cooked, or even the whitish liquid produced when it was being made. They drank it mixed with saccharine. After a certain period of time their faces swelled up. When I saw people with puffy faces tottering towards the house, I knew that was what they were coming for. Shortly after that we too had to start eating pine bark.

People generally died at night, and every morning we counted five or six deaths in our neighbourhood. Most of them were ordinary people, because neither cadres nor policemen nor high-ranking military officers suffered as a result of the famine. My father calculated that the district where we lived had shrunk from four thousand to two thousand inhabitants. Most of them died of hunger or diseases related to weakening. The others fled to China. There were empty houses everywhere. We felt as though we were living in a ghost town. Nonetheless, at the time, with my boy's eyes, I found it all relatively . . . normal. It was all I had ever known, and I thought that things abroad must be pretty much the same, or worse, as our leaders told us, assuring us that North Korea was 'paradise' compared to other states. My belief in Kim Il-Sung and Kim Jong-Il remained unshakeable.

5

Survive!

Rat hunting

We hunted rats in the autumn. You need a fair amount of expertise and a high degree of skill to trap the brown or striped rodents that run in our mountains. With Choljin, Kuanyok, Kuanjin and other friends, we set a fire at one of the entrances to their holes, and waited for the smoke to have its effect. An accomplice harpooned the lithe creature with an iron hook the moment it left its lair. Some of my friends ate this particular form of game prepared in a stew, and thought it was delicious. As for me, I preferred to settle for the abundant stores that the far-sighted beast had set by for the future. With shovels and hoes we dug the ground to uncover the network of galleries filled with corn cobs and rice that the animal had stored up.

Survive!

The rat is a highly organised animal. The entrances to its tunnels are protected by straw, which keeps out the cold wind, and extend down a long corridor leading to antechambers where the rats sleep *en famille*. At the very end, in the most inaccessible part of the lair, the stores of different cereals are kept, ears of maize or wheat, often hidden under dead leaves or straw. Sometimes the rat will have taken the trouble to sort and husk little piles of white rice. Once we had recovered these provisions, we cooked and ate them. Each hole contained at least a handful of rice or maize.

But we weren't content with pillaging the home of our victim. When we caught a rat, we put a piece of string around its neck. As it tried to escape, it would inevitably lead us to another of its hideouts, where it hid other provisions. Some rats had saved nothing, or as good as nothing, while others lived in the lap of luxury. We allowed the rich rats to live, while those hopeless wretches who had put us to such trouble for nothing we killed ruthlessly with stones or spades. On some occasions we also came across little newborn rats. We let them live so that they would work for us when they were grown.

The rats that we caught served another purpose: placed in rudimentary cages that we had made, they attracted sparrowhawks. A slip knot held by a simple mechanism trapped the predator's claws the moment it tried to make off with its prey. We sold the trapped hawks or ate them ourselves.

We also ate grasshoppers, which are delicious fried, as are dragon-flies. Grilled, the flesh of fat dragon-flies tastes a bit like pork. But you can also eat them raw, once head and wings have been removed. Sparrows and quails also ended up in the pot. We caught them with nets set in wooden frames. We played with these birds for ages, with threads tied to their feet, before finally wolfing them down. Other birds, like crows, which we fried on a brazier, were part of our day-to-day life during the famine. Crows have a bad reputation. When you encounter one, you're supposed to spit on the ground to avoid bad luck. My father joined us in these feasts in spite of himself, because crow's meat is considered a tonic for men. It also cures night fevers, my grandmother used to say. On the other hand she advised us not to overdo it: the saying is that if you eat too much *kamagi* (crow), your skin can turn *kama* (black).

But as the vegetation disappeared from the sides of the mountains, which were soon stripped bare by people collecting firewood, the wildlife also began to vanish. When this happened, some people began eating earthworms, and *pidun* (pigweed), which can make your face swell up and even poison you if you eat too much of it. It was not unknown for people in the area to die after eating poisonous mushrooms. Even loaches, the scavenging fish that we caught with nets in the river, started to become scarce as so many starving people were catching them in order to survive.

Survive!

A little distance from the city, trout and salmon were raised for export in the tanks of a State fish farm. Entry was strictly regulated, and the place was very well guarded. But one day a miracle happened. The plentiful spring rain caused the tanks to overflow and dozens of the beautiful gleaming fish spilled over the edges of the brimming pools. It almost caused a riot. In the hours that followed, hundreds of starving people threw themselves like lunatics into the torrents to grab this fabulous booty with their hands, and there was nothing the guards could do about it.

The swallow children

By about 1996, the numbers of beggars thronging the markets had burgeoned. Tired, ragged children wandered through the city. People gave these beggar gangs the name of *chebi* – 'swallow' – because this bird, which leaves in the autumn and comes back in the spring, is constantly in search of warmth and food. First of all there were the *kotchebi*: the very young street children. They were called this because *kot* means 'the bud of a flower'. And Kim Il-Sung, as I have said before, had announced that children were the 'flower-buds of the nation'. Then there were the adolescents, called *chongchebi* (*chong* means 'youth'). Finally, the old people who begged for their food were called *nochebi* (*no* means 'old'). The ones called *kotchebi* were children abandoned by parents who could no longer feed them, or who wandered the streets because there was nothing left to eat at home. Unless they had deliberately left the family home, tired of seeing their parents tearing each other apart in constant arguments over the shortage of food. Since it is traditional in Korea for a husband to expect his wife to cook for him, he would accuse her of mismanaging the household budget, of being lazy . . . and the argument would follow on from that. Famine-related rows were very common.

These were the cause of many marital breakdowns. I remember the case of a friend, a neighbour my own age. His family consisted of his parents and a big brother. His mother went off with a lover who was probably wealthier than her husband, who couldn't feed the family. Although he was only a worker, and both unwell and alcoholic, the abandoned husband had taken it upon himself to look after his two sons all by himself. He started selling cigarettes in the market. But he squandered almost all his modest profits on *soju*. He ended up begging in the streets, before dying of hunger, thin as a rake. Then the older brother set off in search of food, but we learned of his death a few weeks later. My friend managed to survive for another month by stealing at the market, before he too passed away.

I also remember that there was another house, very close to ours, where two brothers constantly fought at mealtimes over which of them had more in his bowl. Sometimes they came to blows, under the panic-stricken eyes of their weeping mother.

The famine encouraged the most selfish kinds of behaviour. My grandmother sold soya dishes and soups, a little trade that helped her to survive. She worked not at the market but in her own home, and customers came to see her there. I remember one father who regularly came to my grand-mother's house in secret to eat his fill far from the eyes of his family. He paid her with sacks of coal that he went and collected in the mines that had been spared from flooding, and urged my grandmother not to mention his visits to anyone. My grandmother preferred to be paid in money, but since this rather special customer had the same surname as us, she treated him sympathetically.

The customers who dropped in at the house sometimes spoke of the prostitution that had spread as a result of the famine, and the presence of wealthy Chinese traders. In many of the towns in the north – the border town of Namyang, but also Chongjin, Wonsan, Hamyung – girls of fourteen or fifteen were selling themselves for practically nothing. Prostitutes risked being sent to a penal labour colony, and recidivists could be sent to prison. Nonetheless, many of them continued to ply their trade, especially with army officers and Party cadres. Most of the cadres also had mistresses, usually widows whose husbands had died of hunger. Everyone knew this, but no one spoke of it; particularly not the legitimate wives of the cadres, who feared that kind of opprobrium more than anything.

The colours of hell

Apart from the market, the station was also a hideout for *kotchebi*. In normal times there was a daily train for Chongjin, but the shortage of petrol and electricity had reduced the rail service to one departure every two weeks. The Onsong–Pyongyang line sometimes took a month to reach the capital – as opposed to five hours under normal conditions. So the station was filled with people waiting for trains that never came. It had turned into a big dormitory, where destitute crowds slept night and day on plastic sheets that they had found who knows where. Skeletal children wandered through the waiting room, all of whom suffered from skin complaints. Some of them were very young: I remember kids of one or two who couldn't even stand upright. They walked on all fours on the filthy floor, picking up whatever they could with their black fingers. They put anything they found into their mouths to see if it was edible. There were so many of them that people no longer paid them any attention. At night some of these children, left to their own devices, slept in the station, and others took refuge in houses deserted by their occupants, who had either died of hunger or left in search of food. But in winter, the station was the favoured spot for these desperate souls. Even if the building was not heated, at least the walls were a shelter against the freezing north wind.

There were more girls than boys among the *kotchebi*, perhaps because girls are hardier. Since they weren't so good at escaping, they tended to beg. Others could be seen wandering around the railway tracks picking up, one by one, any grains of rice or wheat that might have fallen from the wagons. About fifty children from all different backgrounds tried to survive like this, by stealing or begging food around the station. Some of them lay lifelessly on the ground, then dropped dead like flies. People gathered for a few minutes around the body of a child who had just died, as though to witness a spectacle, but then lost interest again almost immediately. In these times of famine, each person thought only of himself. Corpses sometimes stayed where they were for a whole day, amidst the general indifference.

This problem became so acute that the council finally set up a special unit, dependent on the police, with the task of dealing with the *kotchebi*. The members of the unit had a dual function. They had the task of rounding up these 'swallow children' at night, and giving them a meal and a roof to sleep under. But the rations at their disposal were largely inadequate. The children went on dying of hunger, so much so that the unit originally responsible for their wellbeing ended up devoting itself chiefly to the collection and burial of their corpses. A friend of my father, who was part of this group, told us that he never rushed to pick up dead children. He waited until at least two or three had passed away before collecting their bodies in his handcart, because that way he only had to dig a single grave.

The gravedigger often came to see us with his handcarts of inert little bodies, because our house was on the way to the mountain where he dug their graves. He had neither a spade nor a pick, and four or five times a month my father lent him his tools so that he could complete his task. He dug rather shallow graves so as not to tire himself, and then laid the little skeletons in the holes, sometimes without so much as a shroud. On the tumulus, there was never any kind of marker: no name, no sign. The grave disappeared after a while, melting into the bare landscape. The forests had disappeared; even the pines had died, having had their bark torn off to be grated, crushed, boiled in water and then eaten by other starving children. Onsong wore the colours of hell.

Stealing: a matter of life and death

Increasingly, the station and its railway became an essential lifeline for most of the inhabitants of Onsong. Everything was costly. A bun cost five wons, a loaf was ten, a bowl of noodle soup was five wons, and a tofu soup was ten! The workers received their wages less and less often. Many people couldn't feed themselves properly without taking up trading, so thousands of them tried to take the train to buy food less expensively in one place to sell it on elsewhere at a profit. Some of these empty-bellied travellers also relied on being able to borrow money from better-off relations in the city. Since fare-dodgers were liable to be arrested, or even sent to penal labour colonies, it was better to get a travel permit from the relevant office. As a rule, applicants for travel would cite a visit to a sick relative or perhaps a death in the family. The cadres whose job it was to issue these 'permits' turned a blind eye in return for various bribes: a bottle of *soju*, a bag of flour or a bit of money. Since their job had assumed such strategic importance, the cadres of that particular office were easily able to fill their pockets.

So all apprentice traders had to take the train, and it wasn't exactly a picnic. Rail travel in North Korea was such an ordeal that the Party cadres never used this form of transport, choosing cars every time. The carriages always arrived on the platforms packed to the roof, and often a traveller with a valid permit and a ticket would have to wait for a whole series of trains to pass through the station before he was able to board one. Most of the time the doors were blocked by little rascals who made the passengers outside pay to get in. They generally climbed in through the windows, and if you were going to do that it was a good idea to win the co-operation of the passengers already on board by giving them a small gift, such as a bottle of spirits. Once on the train, because of the huge number of passengers the whole journey was spent standing up. The carriages had a stench of poverty, and the toilets swarmed with rats and mice. So lots of people chose to travel along with the fare-dodgers, on the roofs of the carriages, despite the considerable risks. They told themselves there wasn't much to lose.

By 1997, the school had almost ceased to function. Two thirds of the pupils had stopped going to class, and the teachers, who were also dying of hunger, were reduced in number. Our teachers tried to maintain a façade of normality. The institution did everything it could to excuse or ignore the ravages of the famine. Outside of school hours, we were often on 'holiday'. I ended up joining the gangs of children who stole from the market stalls. As the famine got worse, we became increasingly daring. By dint of practice, I became a kind of expert in the art of thieving in an organised gang. My tactic consisted in spotting people who looked well-padded, and hence probably more well-to-do than the average. I had noticed that men generally kept their wallets in their trouser pockets, and women kept theirs in their handbags.

When the potential victim was away from the main drag, I would approach and ask them anodyne questions to distract their attention, things along the lines of 'Where are we?', 'What's the name of this place?' My gang of five or six mates then threw themselves on the person in question and grabbed their money before making off. We sometimes had to use razor blades to cut pockets, and one of us was very skilled at doing that. Then we headed for a suitable place to distribute our booty. Sharing was the rule, and anyone who refused to share was beaten up by the others.

We were taking huge risks. You had to be careful. The task fell to me of assessing our future victims and filtering out 'targets' that were too risky or not worth the trouble. If one of us got caught, solidarity was even more important: all the other gangs of pickpocketing child beggars in the area came to his aid. Sometimes, dozens of us intervened, and we generally got the upper hand, even if it meant tipping over the market stalls. One day, however, one of us fell into the hands of the police. The cops threatened to put him in an orphanage. A catastrophe! Orphanages are real hell-holes, because children don't get fed there, or not much . . . But our friend finally escaped and joined us again. In my gang, everyone thought I was the cleverest and the most clear-sighted. There's no doubt that I did what I did in order to eat, but also to help less clever friends to survive. At least I still had a family and a grandmother who could feed me a little. For many of my friends, on the other hand, stealing was a matter of life and death.

By now people were stick-thin. All were grim-faced and timid, their minds tormented by a single thought: eating to survive. My heart was in my boots as well. At first, hunger is a torture. After that phase you hardly feel a thing. You grow numb, fixated on the stench that sticks to you, the eczema that gnaws at your flaking skin. The misfortune of others, even your own family, leaves you completely indifferent when you have nothing in your belly. Your stomach becomes a thousand times more important than your conscience. You rob ruthlessly, you would even kill. It's that or certain death, the big black hole dug with a spade on the side of the mountain.

6

Fugitive

The revolt

In the autumn of 1997, my father asked the cadres for a change of employment. This was a legitimate request, because he had worked in the mine for more than fifteen years, and the labour had proved to be very hard. Particularly at this time: coal had to be picked up by hand after the dynamite explosions, and the walls had to be dug with picks. My father wanted to become a driver or a mechanic. The cadres refused. My father cited the example of another miner who had just been switched to a less difficult task, but the cadres wouldn't hear of it. 'You have to stay in the mine because Kim Il-Sung and Kim Jong-Il have a great deal of consideration for your work and your family,' they told him. 'What kind of consideration?' my father replied. 'Haven't you been awarded medals?' the cadres asked, 'Letters written in the hand of Kim Il-Sung? Wasn't one of your relations photographed with Kim Jong-Il? These are very great privileges that many people envy you for. The Great Leader and the Dear Leader have a special consideration for your family, and you would be better off showing your gratitude rather than demanding additional privileges.'

My father replied very rudely: 'Our family has done a great deal for the Great Leader, who has done nothing in return. Many times we have sent him medicinal doe horns worth fourteen thousand wons . . . a fortune. Every time we went to Pyongyang, we gave him a present of big baskets of flowers. You talk about consideration, that's fine, but admit it, this consideration isn't really reciprocal! How come I can't change employment when I've been slaving away like a machine for fifteen years? And I'm starting to feel the exhaustion of age.' Then, exasperated by their refusal, my father picked up an ashtray from the desk of one of the cadres, threw it through the window, and started insulting them. He flew into such a rage that he ended up breaking all of the cadres' office windows, calling them fat pigs as he did so!

The comrade cadres decided to make him pay dearly for these insults. They knew very well that there was no point having him arrested by the local police. A member of my father's family had had the privilege of being photographed beside the Great Leader, and his detention would only have touched the hearts of the local police, who would have freed him straight away. So the cadres gave the order to arrest my father at the municipal police headquarters in Onsong, where no one knew him. He would have no special privileges there . . . My dad spent thirteen days in one of the cells in police headquarters, infested with fleas and lice.

At the same time, the cadres threatened to have my father condemned to four years in a work camp. But the letters from Kim Il-Sung to our family constituted a 'mitigating circumstance', so the proposed punishment was reduced to two years. He was to be sentenced to two years in a *rodong danryeondae* (penal labour colony).

In line with the regulations, my father was temporarily released from custody, and summoned to the penal labour colony in Onsong the following week to hear the verdict and begin his sentence. In North Korea, where everyone keeps an eye on everyone else, in normal times no one would have dreamed of trying to get out of such a summons, let alone fleeing the country. But my father, who knew the extreme conditions within the colony at the height of the famine, decided to go for broke and escape to China.

For the sake of caution, he had said nothing of his

decision to anyone, not even my mother. But I suspected that he was up to something, because the day before his departure we ate the rabbit that I was rearing, which I had been saving up for months for some special occasion. After this delicious meal, my father took me aside to advise me always to obey my mother . . . When he returned three months later he told me in detail of his time on the run. It was then that I realised the risks that he had taken.

My father was accompanied on his flight by a friend who had deserted his barracks, where the soldiers barely had anything to eat. If caught, a deserter risked facing the firing squad. So the two men had put their heads together and come up with the idea of crossing the Tumen, the river that separates North Korea from China. It was at points where it was fordable or frozen that many fugitives tried to cross the river, and also where the guards were most numerous and most vigilant. So my father and his friend had gone for the most dangerous place, where the river was very deep and the current very strong. There, a vast number of fugitives had been swept away by the whirling currents, intensified by the barriers built along the banks. After a long period of hesitation, my father told me, they both stripped, tied their clothes to their backs and threw themselves into the freezing water. Struggling against the current that was dragging him away, my father was suddenly seized with a fit of cramps, and only found the will to overcome the pain, he told me, by thinking about my mother and me. Having reached the opposite shore, he and his companion wrung out their clothes, put them back on and, chilled to the bone, made their way to the nearest village.

In prison

In China, my father did all kinds of jobs that he didn't tell me about in detail. But he insisted that over there everyone had plenty to eat. After three months, and after saving some money, he decided to come back. His plan was to come and get me and my mother, and bring us back to China. But he was stopped on a path not far from the Chinese border, having just crossed the Tumen back into North Korea. He was laden with sausages and foodstuffs, which he was carrying in a bag over his back, meant for us. A soldier aimed a pistol at him, and at first my father lied, saying that he was coming back from Namyang, near the border. Seeing that the soldier didn't believe him, he offered him cigarettes and money. But the man would have none of it and, as night was falling, brought him to an army camp. In a big room lit by oil lamps, the officers opened his bag and took out the food, which they wolfed down before his very eyes. Always quick to anger, my father couldn't bear to see this treasure, which he had taken such trouble to amass and transport, being devoured right in front of him. He protested, fists flew, and the officers, infuriated, beat him to calm him down. He was transferred to a larger barracks and then, the following morning, several soldiers and an officer escorted him on foot to the security office in Onsong, about twenty kilometres away.

Their path took them along the river Tumen, and on a number of occasions my father tried to seize the opportunity to escape. He thought that the guards didn't have real bullets in their rifles, only blanks. In fact, an incident that had occurred several months earlier not far from there had led the hierarchy to prohibit real bullets; some starving North Korean soldiers had crossed the border to steal food and, when they were caught by the inhabitants, had killed a number of them. China had protested, and from that point onwards demanded that the Korean troops guarding the shore be incapable of firing on Chinese citizens again. So my father tried to get to the bank to throw himself in the water, but his escort called him to order every time he did so, and he wasn't able to give them the slip.

He reached the security office on New Year's Day. The police, who had had a fair amount to drink to celebrate the occasion, put him in a corner and gave him a good kicking, swigging as they did so. The next day, my father was trans-ferred to Onsong prison, where he underwent a fortnight of severe questioning about his activities in China.

My father described to me how the prison was surrounded by a wall made of breeze-blocks about one metre eighty centimetres tall, topped by pieces of broken bottle and an electrified fence. A guard made him undress, take off his belt and even the elastic of his underpants. No metal was allowed, so all the zip fasteners in his clothes were unstitched and removed. Some prisoners actually swallowed objects, even zips or buttons, so that they would need an operation in a hospital outside the prison: if that happened, they had a much greater chance of escape.

A guard then took my father to his cell, which had a tiny door; the prisoners called the opening 'the niche door'. You had to crouch down to get in, and then the guard kicked you in by the backside. There were ten cells in Onsong prison, five reserved for men and five for women. The cells were really meant for seven people, but all of them held at least twenty. Unlike my father, all of his cell-mates were prisoners who had already been condemned to *kam-ok* (prison), while he was simply in *ku-ryu-jang* (remand for questioning). Sentenced prisoners aren't gen-erally there for very long, for they rarely survive more than a few years in prison.

The prisoner who was the cell leader gave my father another search to be sure that he wasn't hiding anything on his person, then read him the regulations and delivered his report to the guard outside. After that, my father had to sit down on the floor with the others, in line with the regulations: in a row, cross-legged, with their hands under their legs, facing the bars of the tiny 'niche door', their heads tilted at an angle of forty-five degrees, and without moving or speaking. According to the rules, all prisoners lose their status as citizens, and are therefore forbidden to express themselves either by words or movement. The prisoner loses his identity and becomes a mere number. By the same logic, a person in prison is excused from politics classes: because he is not part of society, there is no point in re-educating him. This is not the case in the *kyohwa so*, the re-education labour camps.

Whenever one of the prisoners moved an arm or lifted his head even a little, he was punished by the leader. The punishment consisted in putting his hands on the bars, which the guard outside then struck with a cane. Anyone who pulled his hands back to avoid the cane received an additional series of blows. Many of the prisoners treated in this way lost several fingernails.

Rations in prison were reduced to a bowl of seventy grams of thick maize porridge accompanied by a ladleful of clear soup, three times a day. The porridge was served in tiny plastic bowls, but to make it last longer some prisoners kneaded it with their hands and put it in a rolled-up plastic sheet, sucking out the contents one mouthful at a time. The others used a special aluminium spoon without a handle, which came with the bowl. Detainees who had been imprisoned for fleeing to China, where they had become used to eating well, did everything they could think of to obtain extra rations – many of them sold the new, modern Chinese clothes that they were wearing (a fashionable t-shirt was exchanged for fifteen rations) so a kind of trade was established between the captives and their warders. But this kind of commerce could be harmful because there was no electricity or heating, so jettisoning some of your clothes wasn't a brilliant idea. For some people it was a choice between dying of hunger or dying of cold.

Just after his arrival at mealtime, a guard said to my father, 'Because you've been in China, where you've put on weight, you will fast for three days.' In Onsong my father had a reputation as a brawler. He had even been nicknamed 'the terrible'. And let's not forget, one of the members of our family had had his photograph taken with Kim Il-Sung! When he found out who he was dealing with, the guard ended up giving my father favourable treatment. He was allowed to sit at the back of the cell where there wasn't so much of a cold draught. He also had one of the six blankets that the nineteen other detainees shared to sleep all to himself.

Everyone in the prison had to get up at five o'clock in the morning, and the day began with the cleaning of the floor of the cell and the toilets. As there was no water, excrement had to be taken away by hand. After that the prisoners took up their cross-legged position again, and had to remain silent and motionless. This was real torture, because while the lice ate you up, all you could do was watch them go about it, since the slightest movement was punished. My father's clothes were tight at the cuffs, so the lice, unable to get any further, congregated on that part of his body and bit him to pieces. Years later, my father still bears the marks . . .

Only once a day, the prisoners enjoyed a break during which they were allowed to move. It lasted ten minutes. The prisoners, whose legs were often swollen and puffy because their blood circulation stopped almost completely in that cross-legged position, could barely get to their feet. They tried to do exercises, but their main activity consisted of killing lice. The parasites had laid so many eggs that their clothes were white inside. On the day that my father arrived he had thought that his cellmates had dandruff, but he soon worked out that it was really nits. The

140

adult lice were completely black, so gorged were they with blood.

At night, a makeshift light burned: a little bulb plugged into a car battery. It went out at eleven o'clock. In line with the regulations, the prisoners slept head to foot, to keep them from talking to one another. They had just enough room to lie on their side, and spent the night crammed like sardines. They were packed so close together that if one of them got up to do his business, when he returned he couldn't find a space and had to sleep in a crouching position for the rest of the night. Even in these circumstances no one would have dared to wake up his cellmates. In fact, it was better not to annoy anyone, especially the *kambanzhang*, the cell leader. Generally chosen for his brutality and lack of scruples, he could deprive a prisoner of food, if he felt like it, on grounds of bad behaviour. This meant that he had the power to decide on the life or death of his fellow prisoners.

My father was regularly called for questioning, before returning to the collective cell. Despite the harshness of the regime, he was able to chat to some of his companions in misery. Mealtimes were best for that. My father realised that almost all the prisoners were there for hunger-related crimes. One of his neighbours confessed to him that he dug up dead people to pump out the liquid inside their brains with a syringe. He was able to sell it at a high price, since popular wisdom attributed medicinal virtues to the 'extract'. It was to that kind of madness that people were driven by famine.

Cannibalism

One day, a new prisoner, a man in his thirties, was thrown in through the niche door. Some of his ribs were broken. The police had tied him to the radiator and kicked and punched him. This kind of treatment wasn't very common, so it provoked a degree of curiosity. By way of explanation, the newcomer lied at first, saying that he had been imprisoned for stealing meat. But his story didn't hold up. He finally told his cellmates the true version of events.

While his wife had gone away for a few days in search of food, he had stayed at home with his eight-year-old daughter. She had endlessly demanded food from him, but he had nothing to give her, and he himself was tortured by hunger. An argument broke out, tempers frayed and he hit the girl, whose head struck the ground. She was unconscious, he said, and white foam was coming out of her mouth. He figured that she hadn't long to live, and if she survived she risked having a serious illness. So he decided to finish her off and eat her. He went and got his axe, broke her skull, and began by stripping the flesh from her arms. Having consumed that over a period of several days, he started on the flesh of her thighs and her legs, then her liver. Once this terrible feast was over, the man burned the rest of the body in the stove of the house to get rid of it. He scattered the ashes and the charred pieces of flesh in the mountains. But some time later, a dog came back to the village with a piece of human bone. The police inquiry made the connection with the man's daughter, since he had announced her disappearance, made him confess his crime, beat him up and threw him in jail, where he was now awaiting trial.

As his broken ribs caused him pain, the cannibal couldn't even sit down, so he remained in a lying position. He gradually weakened so much that he could no longer eat. He was forever calling for water, but the prisoners were not allowed to drink anything apart from their three daily ladlefuls of soup, and the guards replied to his requests with a series of insults. Without water he was unable to eat, so he put his ration in his pockets. He contracted terrible diarrhoea and was reduced to trying to drink his own urine. When his breathing became very weak, the other prisoners, seeing his condition, immediately diagnosed that he was in his death-throes. 'We're used to it,' they told my father. At a sign from the cell leader, the prisoners leapt on the dying man to take his clothes, the rations he had hidden in his pockets and his shoes. My father rebuked them: 'How can you do something like that to a sick man?' 'He's going to die anyway, and his clothes won't be much use to him then, but the living have to go on living!' they replied.

The man gave up the ghost the following day. Seeing the corpse, the cell leader got up and, facing the door, formally declared, in accordance with prison regulations: 'Cell number seven has a report to make: prisoner number eight has died.' The guard came in and assigned five prisoners to take the corpse away. They took him by his feet and dragged him out of the cell and into the corridor. My father said he could hear the dead man's head knocking against the floor and the doorposts.

While my father was in prison, two prisoners died of hunger in his cell within the space of a fortnight. Families were never informed of the death of a relation in prison, and if the relative of a dead man turned up, the guards simply told them, 'There's no point looking.' Everything was done to ensure that graves could not be found, because the prisoner, no longer holding the status of a citizen, simply vanished, without flowers or wreaths.

In Onsong, the burial of prisoners took place as follows: the guards led the fellow detainees, who carried the corpse out of the prison, to the maize fields, which were terraced down the hillside. Some distance away, there were dozens of holes, about fifteen metres deep, dug by the inhabitants in search of coal. Whole families broke their backs in them to bring back coal, which they carried up in little baskets. These private mines were only just tolerated, and the authorities had the right to confiscate any coal from them. The guards chose a very deep hole and ordered the people working in it to put the corpse inside and then block up the pit, which was now a grave. This was always done without the knowledge of the dead person's family, who stood no chance of ever finding the remains of their relative: they would never be able to commune with them by their graveside, because there was no graveside. However, in Onsong the family of one person who had been executed did manage, doubtless by handing over a few bribes, to find the victim's grave. But they were promptly dispatched to the penal labour colony.

Another cannibal was incarcerated in cell number nine of the prison my father was in. His surname was Moon, and he was over sixty. He had confessed to the police that he had eaten over forty women, whom he had chosen because they were slightly plump. Sentenced to death, he had nothing left to lose, and had made up his mind to escape. One day, at mealtime, he discreetly sharpened the aluminium spoon that came with the bowl and slashed his neck and the veins of his arm. In hospital, he thought, he might have a chance of escaping. But the opportunity never arose. A doctor stitched up his wounds, and he was brought back to his cell under special guard.

Since all was lost, the serial killer told the story of how he went about perpetrating his crimes. In the daily market in Onsong, he circled around the women who came from out of town to sell maize. He lured them to his house, assuring them that he had large quantities of maize that he wanted to get rid of. When the victims leaned over a barrel of maize that he kept in his storeroom, he hit them in the back of the head with an axe. After cutting them up Moon, along with his mother, who was over eighty, and his son ate them. His son was married, but his wife refused to touch human flesh. Nonetheless, she did keep the terrible secret. The last of Moon's victims was a woman from the neighbourhood, and that was his mistake. He had killed the wife of one of his old schoolmates. The man's suspicions were aroused, and he finally discovered the Moon family's macabre secret. The killer, his son and his old mother were sentenced to death. Only the daughter-in-law, who had not eaten human flesh, was released.

To make an example of them, the police organised a sinister 'harsh critique' of the accused. With police on either side, they were dragged by their feet through Onsong for a whole afternoon, adorned with evidence of their crimes. The grandmother had to wear a plate on her head bearing the decomposed skull of a victim, while the murderer and his son had pieces of charred human remains tied around their necks. They wore them pitifully, heads lowered, under the insults of the population, who pelted them with stones. This unforgettable scene took place in late August or early September of 1997. The grandmother and the son were executed soon afterwards, but the killer, after spending a long time in prison waiting for the order of execution to be issued by the cadres examining his file in Pyongyang, finally starved to death in his cell.

The penal labour colony

After a fortnight in that prison, my father was sentenced to six months of re-education through labour. My mother and I knew nothing of this at the time. He was transferred to the camp in Onsong to serve his sentence. Every town in North Korea has a *rodong danryeondae*, more commonly called a *kopac*. The Onsong *kopac* was reserved for escapees and those who stole from the fields to eat. There were about a hundred prisoners there, both men and women. The penal labour colony was surrounded by a two-metre-high wooden fence topped with barbed wire. At the entrance, my father told me he recognised one of the guards. They had often drunk together, and my father tried to fraternise with him. But the guard acted as though he didn't know him, and walked over to him to strike him around the head. The director of the *kopac*, who was a distant relation of my mother's, reacted similarly. My father begged him to excuse him from work, showing his arms and his hands, swollen by the now septic louse bites. But he would hear nothing of it.

Men and women were separated inside the camp, but they went out to work together. The main task consisted of using their spades to dig an air-raid shelter not far from the camp. This was exhausting work, because the earth was frozen. They worked from seven o'clock in the morning until seven in the evening. Sometimes they also had to do excavation work in the barracks, make breeze-blocks or repair pipes that had burst in the frost. In the morning, after roll-call, the prisoners came out of the camp to go to work, surrounded by armed guards who kept them under constant surveillance. When they came back in the evening, they were made to sing the song 'Let us safeguard socialism'. Then came another roll-call, followed by an hour and a half of political studies.

These sessions, my father told me, were generally the most detested, because the prisoners had been slaving away all day on an empty stomach, and all they could think about was their evening meal. For political studies, the detainees had to sit down in a row and read texts by Kim Il-Sung and Kim Jong-Il on the ideology of *juché*, and learn some of them by heart. Those who were unable to memorise the texts were severely punished. In the winter, when the temperature often drops to minus twenty or minus thirty degrees, they were forced to walk around the courtyard, feet and hands bare, chanting the passages that they were supposed to remember, until they were able to recite them unprompted.

After this study session, the prisoners finally ate their rather disgusting meal, which consisted of clear soup, three or four maize cobs and a bowl of *susu*, a kind of rice straw usually used to make brooms, mixed with scraps of crushed corn cob that was normally fed to pigs. There were three meals, and the regulation weight of the ration in the penal labour colony was two hundred grams, while it was only seventy grams in prison. The meal was followed by another study session, which lasted until eleven o'clock in the evening. Anyone who refused to obey was put in chains and shackled to a post.

Some of the old people in the camp died relatively quickly. One of the most frequent causes of death was constipation, brought on by the kind of food that they were made to eat. It's a horrible death. Many people died shortly after leaving the camp, no doubt from exhaustion, and also because in many cases they had absolutely nothing to eat once they returned home. Paradoxically, for the poorest people, the camp offered a better chance of survival than the outside world did. Some even joked that they would rather eat in the labour colony than die in freedom . . .

Typhus

My mother had been alerted to the fact that my father was in the camp by some security men who asked her to bring him a change of clothes. When she recovered my father's rags, they were infested with bugs, fleas and lice. Family visits were permitted once a day for a duration of thirty minutes, at lunchtime. The few people who could afford to do so brought the prisoner they were visiting food, which was precious because it was very hard to survive on the miserable rations allowed by the authorities in the labour colony.

When I visited, my father had a very high fever so couldn't choke down the food that my mother and I had brought him. He fasted for nine days, which weakened him considerably. A nurse in the colony brought him to hospital for tests; he had his temperature taken, he had blood tests, and the doctors diagnosed typhus. I realise now that my father must have contracted the disease from the lice that had devoured his wrists. But at the time, I believed the official explanations of the causes of the ailment: this kind of contagious illness, according to the propaganda, very often comes from South Korea, the source of all evils. Likewise, we were told that you could catch cholera by eating sea-fish – which is false, as I now know – and that infected fish 'obviously' came from South Korean waters. I can remember a period in 1997 when cholera wrought havoc and the population had been officially forbidden to eat sea-fish. In any case, the fish were beyond our price-range, and only the most affluent were able to afford them.

Given the risk of infection in the municipal labour colony, where half the prisoners already suffered from the same illness, my father was granted exceptional permission to leave the camp, on the express condition that he would come back if he survived and was able to get back on his feet. In line with the procedure in such cases, he was put back into the hands of our local police, who escorted him home. Dad was with us again! But that didn't mean he was free. The police paid him daily visits, and the local committee, as well as all our neighbours, had been mobilised by security to keep an eye on him. So in the course of the day, about ten informers of all kinds came regularly to our house to spy on everything we did. Each of them had to deliver a daily report to the security services.

I was in my second year of secondary school at the time, and the atmosphere had become unbearable. Some of my fellow pupils had started calling me 'son of a traitor to the nation'.

I fought with them. The other children whose parents had
fled to China, escapes being by now quite common, were
all bullied and insulted in the same way. One day, the son of
a cadre told me that his father had seen mine in the labour
colony shackled in chains. He provoked me and, once again,
I fought back violently. The other pupils tried to intervene,
and then the teacher arrived. He said to me, 'And here you
are, fighting on top of everything else . . . When your father
is in the state he's in. That just tops everything!' His remark
cut me to the quick, and I went home straight away. I stayed
there for a few days before returning to school. It was my
grandmother who made me go back; I was really reluctant
to do so. When I got there it was even worse than before.
Everyone gave me dirty looks. I was now, quite clearly, the
'Chinese traitor'. All those idiots disgusted me.

After that I flat out refused to go back to school, and this
time my grandmother understood. She stopped insisting.
Anyway, it didn't matter all that much any more: four
pupils had died of hunger, and most of the others were too
weak even to show up. All these factors put things in per-
spective for me. I started wondering what was really
important in life.

My father recovered gradually from his typhus. It was
during his convalescence that he told me of his misadven-
tures in prison and in the labour colony. And he knew that

the sooner his health recovered, the sooner he would have to go back to the *kopac*. Depressed, he hit the bottle. When he was drunk on *soju*, he sometimes said much more than you really wanted him to. One evening, he suddenly started shouting at the top of his voice: 'Kim Jong-Il, son of a bitch . . . bastard, swine!' My mother, in a panic, threw herself at him, jamming both hands over his mouth. My grandmother, who was also in the room, was utterly horrified. She went out to keep an eye on our neighbours and check that they hadn't heard anything. If they had, we would very likely have been reported, and the whole family would have faced the firing squad.

On another occasion, when he had drunk more than usual, my father started shouting, 'Even the dogs in China eat better than we do! Even the poor eat white rice! That's where we've got to go!' My mother and I tried to shut him up. 'If you don't come with me, I'll kill you both before I go!' he yelled.

Leaving!

My father had made his mind up: he would take my mother and me to China. From that moment, every day for more than a month, we argued about whether or not we were going. My father tried everything he could think of to persuade us: 'Even the poorest eat rice in China,' he repeated, but my mother wasn't convinced. 'In spite of the shortages,' she replied, 'North Korea is without a doubt one of the most prosperous countries in the world! And anyway, what would happen to the rest of the family if we escaped? Go on your own!' But my father insisted: 'Even if you die I'll take you to China. You have to see how things are over there. If you don't like it, you can always come back!'

My father's arguments didn't wash with me either. I told him I would rather be a beggar in North Korea than follow him to China. I replied in set phrases that I had learned at school, along the lines of 'Let us safeguard socialism', or 'I will fight to the death to protect socialism and the Great Leader Kim Il-Sung!'

Finally my father said to me, 'You know, Hyok, if I go back to the camp I will die.' That made me think, although it did nothing to shake my determination. My father, who was delirious because of his illness, went on insulting Kim Jong-Il in the worst possible terms, calling him a 'dirty dog' and accusing him of sleeping with all the women in the country . . . I was really confused, not least because now more than ever, in those hungry times, state propaganda went on singing the praises of the 'Great and Invincible Leader'. As I have said, I had stopped going to school. It was my decision, but I should also point out that, given my state of mind, and since my father was worried that I would report him to my classmates, he himself had forbidden me to go.

My mother finally yielded to my father's insistence. In turn, she tried to persuade me to follow them. 'You can't survive here, eating nothing but maize noodle soup!' she said to the little thirteen-year-old boy that I was at the time. She added that we would spend a year in China, no more, and that we would earn money and come back to North Korea. Reluctantly, I finally agreed.

People came discreetly to give us tips on the best escape routes, and my father swapped information with them as well. But we had to be on our guard against the plainclothes security agent specially assigned to keep watch on us. He would suddenly drop in on us to 'chat', as he said, and sound out our intentions. To reassure him, my father exaggerated the pain he was suffering from a septic wound in his leg and his buttock, and pretended to limp. The security agent doubtless deduced from this that even if my father did want to escape again, his handicap would prevent him from doing so.

For the sake of prudence, it was better not to talk of our departure for China except when we were in the house. But even within our own four walls we whispered, trying never to mention the words 'leaving' or 'China'. We had to be very careful, to be sure that no one suspected a thing. My father made a point of telling all the neighbours that he hadn't the slightest intention of going back to China, it had cost him too much already. By saying these things he tried to free himself of any suspicions. Even at the age of thirteen, it seemed to me that that kind of declaration was just as likely to awaken doubts as it was to allay them.

For my part, I didn't want to leave without saying goodbye to my three best friends. I slipped off to see Choljin, Kuanyok and Kuanjin on the sly. I revealed the secret of our imminent departure, and all four of us cried. As I left them, I gave them a present of my most precious belonging, the collection of songs that I had illustrated and bound myself. Then we swore we would see each other again one day.

The escape

We made our getaway on 19 March 1998 at four o'clock in the morning. Our decision had been made the previous day, at the home of my maternal grandmother. We had to leave well before sunrise, because that was the time when my father was under the least amount of surveillance. I remember that my grandmother hadn't been able to get to sleep, and that she was still up when we awoke. She tearfully gave us some pieces of tofu. 'Build your strength up, you're going to need it!' she advised. But we could hardly get anything down.

My mother had saved three hundred wons, just in case

our attempt failed, because then we would have to pay some smugglers to help us. We had only the clothes on our backs, because even the smallest bundle of clothing would have looked suspicious. In two hours we travelled the twelve or so kilometres that separated us from the border. There were eight of us in all. My father, my mother, a friend of my aunt's, two of my father's friends, one of whom had brought his son and daughter along, and me. We reached the river Tumen at seven in the morning. It was minus twenty degrees . . .

We got ready to cross the border at a ford, walking carefully on the ice. My father was with me, as well as my mother and the five other fugitives. It was at that point that the border guards appeared, brandishing their rifles. They headed towards our little group of runaways. For the first time in my life I was really frightened. I was the first to run on to the frozen river. I fell, I got up, I took a few steps, then I slipped again before losing my balance and falling into the icy water . . . I swam without looking back, I fought my way between the blocks of ice, my body freezing, my heart beating a hundred times a second. The soldiers who were chasing us yelled at us to stop, to come back. They didn't shoot . . . Were they taking time to aim? Maybe they didn't have any bullets? One sole thought inspired me now, hammering at my temples: get away from them . . . flee at any cost. I felt like a hunted animal.

This Is Paradise!

And now I was running on the bank on the other side of the river, frantic, breathless, stunned. It was unimaginable: I had crossed the border! My father ran behind me, along with five others. My mother was still in the water, so I helped her on to dry land, then she pushed me towards the bushes for cover. The furious soldiers watched after us for a while from the opposite shore, threatening us with their rifles. We were so happy to have crossed over that we mocked them for not even having any ammunition in their weapons. Dad and I yelled, 'Come and catch us if you can!' and punctuated our words with obscene gestures.

7

China

A frog out of the pit

We arrived at the edge of a village where my father knew someone: a Chinese man of Korean origin whom he had met after his previous crossing. When he saw us in the distance, so many of us, all drenched to the bone, the Chinese man immediately worked out where we had come from.

'Whatever you do, don't stay here!' he said. 'If there's a check we'll be fined.' (The Chinese authorities fine anyone who gives shelter to North Korean fugitives.) Then, afraid that some passers-by might see us, he ushered us into his house where we dried ourselves a little. As our clothes were lined to keep out the winter cold, the water had made them very heavy. The man gave me a bowl of rice, then cakes and candies. I was so surprised by his kindness. In North Korea, no one would have done that. My father said to me, 'You see, they have rice over here!' I ate without a word. The man even gave my mother a pair of trousers as she had torn hers during our escape.

For greater safety, we had waited for sunset before entering the village. Just as we were about to make our minds up, a man on a motorcycle arrived. We all thought it was a policeman come to arrest us. But fortunately no, it was another ethnically Korean Chinese man.* 'You should have crossed earlier! You will be noticed and reported straight away,' he said when he saw us there, our clothes still wet. 'And the little boy must be cold, he'll catch his death,' he added, looking me up and down.

In the village, we crept past the house of a woman with a baby on her back, who was selling grilled meat. The smell made my mouth water. She immediately offered me a piece of her delicious meat. I was dumbfounded. I couldn't understand such generosity. One surprise after another. I later worked out that this tradeswoman had guessed from our appearance that we were fugitives: that was the only reason for her generous gesture.

----

*In China, people who speak Korean are seen as an ethnic minority.

China

I was astonished by the number of cars driving about this Chinese village, by the shop-windows filled with food and by the prosperity of the people who lived there. On a greengrocer's stall, I discovered the existence of bananas and clementines. I'd never seen anything like them before. They lived well in China, people were well fed, and some of them had fat, oily faces. Back in Korea, there was only one obese person in the whole country: Kim Jong-Il!

Lovers held hands in the street, women wore short skirts, trousers and low-cut tops under their nylon anoraks. How curious it was to see people doing whatever they felt like, and wearing whatever they liked! In North Korea, women had to wear skirts below the knee, men had to close their shirt-collars and, most importantly, wear a portrait of Kim Il-Sung or Kim Jong-Il on their clothes at all times. Here, everyone looked relaxed, and the people wore spontaneous expressions on their faces. Many of them expressed themselves exuberantly, and went about their business with an energy that I had never seen in North Korea. I suddenly realised the extent to which people back home always looked as though they were wearing a mask. Here, everything seemed, how can I put it . . . authentic. My father whispered in my ear: 'You see, in China, you just have to work to live well . . .'

It all left me terribly confused. I began to realise that what I had learned in North Korea wouldn't be of much use to me on this other, weird planet. I felt like a frog that had just come out of its pit, from which it had contemplated the circle of sky outlined by the rim, and taken it for the whole of the world. I had passed through to the other side of the mirror.

We took a bus away from the border, towards the nearest large town. At that moment, four years of optimism began for us. But we were constantly haunted by the fear of being stopped by the Chinese police, who automatically and forcibly repatriated all North Korean 'illegal immigrants'.

My father had several jobs in China. He started out working in a sawmill, and then he worked as a waiter in a restaurant where my mother sometimes did some cooking. A little paradise for us, after the famine. Then my father helped a Chinese man from Shandong province install machines in a studio, before going off to prospect for gold in Jinchang, in a private mine. Gold-bearing land abounded in the mountains of Manchuria. The owner of the goldmine, Mr Chen, had no problems about hiring my father. We were vaguely related to him, because a cousin of my mother's, who had fled to China shortly before we did, had married a Chinese member of his family.

Seeing me, Mr Chen told my father that it was a shame

In the collective fields, the army had orders to shoot
on sight. We stole to eat, but at great risk to ourselves

At the time, my image of happiness was eating
the ears of maize that we had just
stolen after school

In order to economise, we ate noodles that my
mother boiled down for a long time until they
became a clear soup

When I was at primary school, the moment we
broke up for the holidays I went to scrape coal
in the mines to exchange it for food

We went rat hunting in the autumn. A certain amount of know-how and a large amount of skill were required to trap the brown or striped rodents that ran wild in our mountains

This woman, in Onsong market, yelled, 'You rat! I can't even feed myself. How dare you steal from me?'

With some of my class, I went to the home of our friend who had died of the famine. Her grandmother wept by her lifeless body

I remember there was another house, very close to my own, where two brothers argued endlessly at mealtimes over who had more than the other in his bowl

When I was nine, I saw my first execution in the
grounds of the brick factory

In China, my father treated my mother, who
suffered from back pains. We couldn't afford
to buy medication

In September 2000, we were arrested by the Chinese police. We risked being repatriated to North Korea. My parents pleaded: 'Take us, but leave our son!'

We had to work like galley slaves for bosses who were often haughty, and quite capable of reporting us to avoid paying our wages

To get from China to Vietnam, in late May 2001, we had to cross jungle-covered hills along paths of slippery mud

Some Cambodian border guards spotted us. At rifle-point, they took what little money we had left. We even had to part with our shoes. That was in August 2001

I wasn't going to school. This man, who had a reasonably affluent lifestyle, was very highly respected, and the Chinese police left him alone. He was a good protector. He found me a place at the school in his village by pretending that I was Chinese. I had been in China for several months, and my spoken Chinese had considerably improved. I was soon one of the best pupils in the class. Mr Chen was proud of me. To pay for my schooling, we had also been helped by a teacher who lived in Yanbian. He was part of a support committee that took in hungry North Korean children. He saw that I was good at drawing, and thought of trying to get me into Yanbian art school. He gave up in the end, though, for fear of being arrested.

I had friends at school in China, but we were never very close, because for the sake of caution I had to pass myself off as Chinese. And at first that was by no means easy! I said I came from a village close the North Korean border, which provided a plausible excuse for my poor knowledge of the language, because in that region the inhabitants speak Korean and very bad Chinese. But I couldn't tell my classmates about my past in North Korea. If that terrible secret had come to light, I would have been forcibly repatriated. And anyway, I wanted to forget that terrible period in my life.

I changed school many times, because we were constantly

moving house at very short notice, from one day to the next even, to avoid the police and informers. For that reason I was never able to spend more than six months in a single establishment. But nonetheless, after three years I started making very satisfactory progress in Chinese. To make my cover even more credible, I made a point of not meeting any of my North Korean compatriots. In any case, I didn't bump into them in the schools that I went to because the families of illegal immigrants had neither the leisure nor the desire to send their children there. The important thing for them was to work to live, and that was all there was to it. I was a kind of exception to that rule. I very much wanted to study, to be like the other children of my own age, but also to decode this world, so different from the one I had known.

In China, however, I did things that I'm not proud of now. Without my parents' knowledge I joined a gang of bad boys. At first I just did it for fun and out of curiosity, though by the end I had become involved in acts of brutality that I now regret. But how could I have known that I would get caught up in a spiral of violence?

It all started in one of the schools I went to. In that part of Manchuria, the communities of Chinese extraction and the Chinese minorities of Korean ethnicity didn't mix. Fights often broke out between the two groups. Being very close-knit, the Sino-Koreans came running the moment one of their own was threatened. They wore pagers on their belts, which beeped to round everyone up if a Korean was in trouble. The gang, who had learned that I was an illegal North Korean, paid me a visit one day to suggest that I join their clan. I accepted. We often spent our afternoons in video-game arcades. As we needed money, we did a bit of racketeering at school. One pupil eventually reported us. The gang went and beat him up, and he ended up in an awful way. I felt terrible remorse over that. But when I tried to leave the group, the gang leaders threatened to report me to the police if I did. I understood that they had me in their power, and that it was precisely because illegal immigrants are vulnerable that they had asked me to join their gang in the first place. Fortunately, we left that town shortly afterwards and I was able to escape their punishment.

Police raids

Every time we saw a policeman, in the street or elsewhere, we hid. We had to remain vigilant at all times. Denunciations were common, because the Chinese authorities offered rewards to informers. People who sheltered North Koreans had to pay very high fines, and very few people, apart from the Chinese ethnic Koreans who were very common in that mountain region, would have risked it. They spoke our language and were often very poor at expressing themselves in Chinese.

Some unscrupulous Chinese bosses employed illegal North Korean workers and then reported them to the police the day before pay day, which meant that they didn't have to give them the wages they owed them. And 'women-smugglers' suggested to the penniless families of illegal immigrants that they sell their daughters or their wives to Chinese widowers or bachelors in the country-side. Rates were between five hundred and three thousand yuans, and many people actually did make deals of that kind. Some young female North Korean illegal immi-grants were simply kidnapped and sold by the smugglers, this time without compensation. They ended up in a vil-lage far away from everything familiar to them and, not speaking the language, they lived locked up most of the time. However, from the stories that I have heard on this subject, I imagine they ended up accepting their fate. At least they had enough to eat. And marriage was a good way for a North Korean woman to obtain Chinese citi-zenship. My mother's cousin, whom I mentioned before, had done just that.

The Chinese police were constantly springing raids, both in the street and in people's houses. Even at night, we heard the sirens of the police cars as they headed in search of North Korean illegal immigrants. We were so afraid of being arrested that when we were at home in each of our little rented flats that we moved between we shut all the doors and windows to give the impression that they were empty. We also had to be careful about spies sent by the North Korean government passing themselves off as refugees: they were sleeper cells with instructions to act when a senior official, or someone else who could create difficulties for Kim Jong-Il, fled. Then their mission was to trap him and forcibly repatriate him, with or without the co-operation of the Chinese authorities. So it was better to have a good cover. In our situation, the best possible thing to do was to live among ethnic Chinese. Moving house was also much safer if we were accompanied by local people. Caution led us to move dozens of times, because as soon as anyone in the neighbourhood began to suspect that we had come from the other side of the border, we immediately packed our bags. Tens of thousands of refugees, like ourselves, had to observe those rules of prudence.

Many North Koreans worked in China for a few months, then returned illegally to North Korea to feed their families. It was essential that they should not be caught on the way back. The North Korean border guards, who were well aware that these refugees were bringing money with them to help their relatives who had stayed behind in North Korea, concentrated all their efforts on them. The booty that they took from these unfortunates was a major source of revenue for them. They do the same thing even today. On the other hand, they don't make as much effort to stop people heading in the direction of China, because there aren't many pickings to be had from them.

At first, the returnees hid their money in the soles of their shoes. But that ruse was quickly discovered, and other methods soon appeared. Women hid banknotes in their vaginas, while men swallowed money in plastic bags or contraceptives just before trying to cross the Tumen or the Yalu, the other border river. But there too the North Korean soldiers quickly found out what was going on. From then on, any fugitives that they caught were subjected to a body search along with a compulsory visit to a supervised toilet. The minimum sentence for a refugee was six months of *kopac*.

Sentenced to death

Comings and goings between China and North Korea became relatively frequent, and information spread. At length my father learned from a refugee from Onsong that a meeting of cadres had been held specifically about him, and that in his absence he had been sentenced to death. The chief accusation against him was that by fleeing to China he had 'dishonoured the relationship of trust between his family and the Great Leaders Kim Il-Sung and Kim Jong-Il'. So my father had become an 'anti-revolutionary traitor'. From that moment, arrest by the Chinese police, which would certainly have been followed by repatriation to North Korea, became a constant source of worry.

And in fact, eventually we were arrested, in September 2000, in Wangching. We were at home when, at eleven o'clock in the morning, dozens of police broke down our door. We had been denounced, and I know who by. Next door to our house there was a restaurant run by a woman whose husband was a policeman. One day that woman had asked my father to do her a favour and fetch her a few buckets of water. My father refused the task because the woman had actually worked out that we were illegal fugitives, and thought she could take advantage of the fact by giving us thankless tasks to do. My father's rebuff had not gone down well with her, and that very evening she grassed on us to the police.

In jail, the police put me in the same cell as my father. He had a defeated look about him. A long time afterwards he told me that he was convinced that he was facing certain death, and that he had decided to take his own life rather than be handed over to the North Korean security services, but my presence with him in the cell had kept him from going through with it. There were six other North Koreans in our cell, waiting like ourselves for their forced repatriation. My mother was imprisoned not far away with the women. The Chinese police often postponed transfers until they had a sufficient quota of prisoners, about ten in all, to escort them across the border in one go. There were already at least seven of us . . . time was of the essence.

At the very last minute, my father finally managed to bribe a Chinese prison official, who agreed to let us out for four thousand three hundred yuans (about five hundred pounds). But my father didn't have that kind of money, so he passed a message outside to Liu, one of his ethnic Korean Chinese friends. He had known him for a long time. Liu had often come to see us in Onsong to trade with us. He knew that my father had received a death sentence in North Korea, and that if he didn't help him, all three of us were looking at a death sentence. Some time previously, Liu had fallen seriously ill, and in order to buy the medicine he needed to take care of himself he had sold his little house. So he had a considerable sum of money at his disposal, and he agreed to lend it to my father, who then began his negotiations with the director of the prison.

My father will be eternally grateful to Liu for lending so much money in good faith, with only his word as a guarantee. Dad wasn't able to pay him back until a year after his escape, when he reached South Korea. Using the small allowance that the South Korean government issues to refugees, he sent Liu four times the sum he had borrowed. Without a doubt, that man had saved my father's life; my mother's and mine as well.

8

Flight to South Korea

Scouting

Since our arrival in China my father had planned to settle
there. He didn't allow the fact that we had been arrested to
change his mind. Nor did it occur to him to try to obtain
asylum in South Korea. In fact we believed that life in
South Korea was so wretched that such a plan would be
absurd, since our heads were still full of the horrors constantly and forcefully peddled to us by Northern
propaganda. Sometimes on North Korean television they
showed images of violent demonstrations in South Korea,
which reinforced our very negative impression of the country. Apart from being even poorer than in the North, as we
were told, the people there lived in constant political tur-
moil, under the brutal repression of a helmeted police

force. North Korean propaganda images of the South were always cropped very tightly, and always looked very shaky. I later learned that this technical device served to mask the modern streets and buildings of the metropolitan cities in the South. Nonetheless, in the background, we could still make out beautiful cars that led us to suspect a world very different from the one presented to us. There was no getting round the fact that the South Korean demonstrators wore good-quality clothes. But I didn't pay much attention to that, and in my mind South Korea remained a kind of 'Great Satan'.

However, in Yanbian, a Chinese border town where many illegal immigrants from the North lived, my father met, more or less by chance, some South Korean agents of the *Angibu* (the Ministry of State Security), who painted him a very idyllic picture of South Korea. When he told them that our family had originally been rather well-regarded by Kim Jong-Il, they suggested helping us get to Seoul. But we had grave doubts about the reliability of their descriptions of the South. In China we had plenty to eat, and we were able to provide for the needs of our family who were still in the North by sending them the money we saved. We passed it on via the many North Koreans who came to work illegally in China. Why would we run the risk of a dangerous journey to South Korea where, as we believed, the people lived in poverty?

We would be even further away from our family in need, and also, by throwing ourselves into the arms of the Southern enemy, we would put the lives of our relations in danger.

At the same time, we met a growing number of Chinese people and refugees with family in South Korea. They assured us that it was a rich, modern country, where you could earn ten times as much money as you could in China. The smart appearance of the few South Koreans that we saw in Yanbian, which contradicted our prejudices, also aroused our curiosity. It corroborated what we had been told by those who boasted of the merits of the South . . .

My father then went back to see one of these moles from the South Korean Security Ministry, who was involved in shady dealings in our district in Yanbian. The Southern agent came straight out and offered him a sum of money in exchange for which he would see about getting me to South Korea! My father and mother would later be able to join me, he assured him. But my father, horrified by such a suggestion, sent him packing: 'So that's it! You want me to sell my son! Don't count on me!'

But increasingly we were living like hunted animals in China. Police raids were growing more and more frequent. After our stay in prison, where we had only just escaped forced repatriation, we realised that the risk of being deported was becoming more and more of a threat from one day to the next. Still suspicious of the enchanting stories we were told about South Korea, my father had the idea of trying to ask for political asylum in Japan, where we still had distant family. Some intermediaries allowed him to take the first steps in that direction, but there was at least a year's wait, if not several years. The Japanese authorities required the presence of my grandmother, who had lived in Japan in her youth. That, they said, was what would enable us to obtain a pass. My father thought the whole thing was too random and risky.

In China we had met up with other members of our distant family who had decided to flee as well. Notably Jin, one of my cousins, with whom I got on very well. He was about twenty-five, brilliant and practical too. In North Korea, he dreamed of only one thing: to go and study at university. He always got excellent marks, so he certainly had the ability to achieve it, but as he was a member of a family – ours – which was now considered disloyal to Kim Il-Sung and Kim Jong-Il, the Party had imposed a veto. Having finished secondary school, Jin should then, like everyone else, have done his thirteen-year military service. A few weeks before he was due to join up, he had joined us in China instead. He had immediately found a job as a carpenter, and was doing very well. The head of the workshop thought highly of him, and even had him lined up to succeed him. A short time before, Jin had also been arrested by the Chinese police, who were preparing to repatriate him. Fortunately, his boss took action and bought Jin's way out. Unable to stand being pursued by the Chinese police, Jin had spent months studying the route he would have to take to get to South Korea. There were many sources of information available in Manchuria: the South Korean Protestant pastors, South Korean government agents, Chinese smugglers . . .

One day, Jin and I reached the decision to try our luck. Once we were in South Korea, if we got there, we would write to our family back in China and tell them how to join us. My father and mother pulled faces. Days of endless discussion followed, before an agreement was reached. In the face of my determination, my parents finally, though reluctantly, let me go. I hadn't really given them a choice. 'Whatever happens, I'm going!' I had said categorically to my father, who was still hoping to come up with an alternative plan. In spite of everything, Jin inspired my parents' trust. But one of my arguments had finally carried some weight too: as I was still a minor there was less of a risk. If I was arrested and repatriated to North Korea I might risk only a few months in a labour colony, after which I would soon rejoin my parents in China. Thus it was decided that I would take the road to South Korea. And I would act as a scout.

The day of the big departure was heart-rending. Long, emotional goodbyes . . . Then I set off on the Beijing train with Jin, along with Moon, one of our former neighbours from Onsong who was also hiding in Yanbian, and who was desperate to start the journey. A friend of my father's also went with us part of the way, although he later backed out, fearful of the growing likelihood of arrest involved in such an expedition. One of our trump cards was that I spoke Chinese well, and that got us out of a number of tight spots.

In Beijing we took another train for Southern China, as far as Nanning, about four thousand kilometres away from our starting-point. From there we travelled to the Vietnamese border.

In search of an embassy

To reach Vietnam we had to cross jungle-covered hills, along paths of slippery mud, walking for hours and hours without knowing for certain that we were going in the right direction. Moon cracked: 'I'm too tired! Let me die here.' We had to persuade her to go on, and sometimes even carry her. That was the hardest part of our journey.

Eventually we reached Vietnam. Everything was improvised. We consulted maps and tried in very bad English to get hold of information for our itinerary, but most of the time we couldn't make ourselves understood. When this happened I did drawings, a bus station if we were looking for one, a railway station . . . And when we wanted to find a South Korean consulate, I drew the flag of South Korea.

We crossed Vietnam from north to south by bus and train, and went and knocked at the door of the South Korean consulate in Ho Chi Minh City, formerly Saigon. An employee received us on the doorstep. 'There's nothing we can do for you here. You will have to find your own way'! So we decided to take the bus to Laos. In Vientiane we once again sought help from the South Korean embassy. This time we had a much better reception. Once again we were told that there was nothing they could do for us. We had to cross into Cambodia illegally, following a particular path. After that we had to take a bus to a border area where smugglers on motorbikes would take us across the border. But we were warned: we had to be extremely careful when crossing the border between Laos and Cambodia.

We set off the next day.

There were many contraband crossings at this particular Laotian border, and we had no difficulty in finding smugglers on motorbikes. But we hadn't explained ourselves very well to the two motorcyclists whose services we had hired, and they took us straight to the border checkpoint! At the sight of the soldiers we gestured wildly to our drivers to turn around. We were within a stone's throw of the sentries, and after a moment's hesitation that seemed to last a century, they did as we asked. I have no idea why the soldiers didn't react. Perhaps we turned back where we had come from just in time, without really attracting their attention. We were still in Laos, but our smugglers had finally worked out that we had no papers and that we had to cross the border illegally. So we made a second attempt the following day after lengthy negotiations about the price of the journey, which had by now gone through the roof. They were asking three hundred dollars! We managed to bring them down to a third of that. The road they took was different from the one the previous day, more chaotic and difficult, and the wheels of the bikes kept getting stuck in muddy fields. And with one final flourish the two smugglers threw us right into the lion's den: another border checkpoint, where this time we were arrested.

We had to follow the border guards, with their guns levelled at us, to an army barracks. Now we were in the hands of the Laotian soldiers, and they began to interrogate us. I took it upon myself to do the talking, and claimed, half in Chinese and half in Korean, that we were South Korean citizens and that we had had our papers stolen. Some of the soldiers had a vague understanding of Chinese, and I wanted to say enough to convince them that we were South Korean, without speaking at such length that I gave myself away. The moment their questions became more precise, I answered in Korean to put them off. I thought that our lives might depend on this confrontation, so when they brought in a Laotian–Chinese interpreter, I started speaking only in Korean, to maintain the hazy climate that was protecting us. I told myself that if these soldiers didn't know who we were or where we were from, they wouldn't know what to do with us, and would release us in the end. The important thing was to appear as stupid as possible. It seemed that the soldiers were in cahoots with our crooked smugglers, who had probably brought us to them in the hope of extracting yet more money. The situation was resolved with a financial agreement. The soldiers set us free, and we finally crossed the border by wading through a stream.

The Cambodian colonel

But our troubles were far from over. Some Cambodian soldiers spotted us and, at rifle-point, took all of our remaining money. We even had to part with our shoes. This confrontation was very tense. Convinced that we still had some money hidden about us, one of them pointed a revolver at my chest. I defied him. 'Go on, fire! Try and fire!' I said in Korean. It was at that moment that a senior officer, a colonel I think, turned up. Instantly the atmosphere changed completely. 'I'm here to help you,' the colonel said to us in English, adding, 'You're North Koreans, aren't you?' I maintained that we were South Korean, and that we wanted to get to the South Korean embassy – I stressed the 'South'. I hurried to show him the sketch of a South Korean flag that I had carefully done. 'I understand,' he replied, and made all three of us climb into his car.

After a few hours' drive, we arrived at his house. He lived in a vast and beautiful estate. Tall palm trees grew in the garden. He let us stay there for three hours. We were in an emotional state somewhere between surprise and fear. Cambodia was a dangerous country for fleeing North Koreans, because relations between King Sihanouk and the Kim dynasty were excellent. Kim Il-Sung had placed a palace in Pyongyang at Sihanouk's disposal, and he had used it since the seventies. In Phnom Penh, where I learned there was a 'Kim Il-Sung Street', North Korea has a large embassy. Needless to say, we felt very uneasy in this country, from which we could just as easily have been forcibly repatriated if we were arrested.

It wasn't easy communicating with the colonel. We could only make ourselves understood with a few words of English, and lots of my explanatory drawings. When we finally deciphered the reasons for his haste to step in and help us, we thought them very dubious. He claimed he was being paid by 'someone' precisely to bring illegal North Korean immigrants to a safe place, and that he received a sum calculated on the basis of the number of refugees that he was able to bring to safety. Only then did we confess to him that we were North Koreans, which of course he knew already: 'Only North Koreans ever pass through here,' he said casually.

In spite of everything, we couldn't be completely certain about the colonel's intentions. When, after three days, he asked us to climb into his car again to go to Phnom Penh, we were very tense. I kept my hand on the door handle the entire time just in case we needed to escape. The road, which was relatively empty, was very straight. Unlike North Korea, there was no one walking along the verge.

In the middle of nowhere, the colonel pulled over. About half an hour later, another vehicle coming in the opposite direction stopped next to ours. Two men with dark glasses got out. The colonel got out to meet them, gesturing to us to stay in the car. I picked up a few phrases in Korean exchanged between these two strangers, and their accents sounded Northern to me. My heart was in my mouth, my hand gripping the door handle. The group moved slightly away, one of the strangers took an envelope out of his pocket, counted the banknotes and gave them to the colonel. It was then that he gestured to us to get out of the car. One of the men in dark glasses dashed towards us: 'How happy we are to see you . . . you're well, I hope . . . all three of you in good health, I hope . . . your long journey is over . . . you're safe now, there's nothing to worry about.'

In the other car, which was taking us who knows where, this man subjected us to a barrage of questions. How long ago had we left North Korea? How much time had we spent in China? Where? One of his questions was repeated three times: Do you go to church? To this very curious question I immediately replied in the negative. In North Korea, I told him, people don't even know what church is. He shook his head, saying, 'Never mind, now, we're going to take you to South Korea.' But I was still wondering whether those two strangers who said they wanted to help us were from North or South Korea.

We crossed a river on a car ferry where there was a police check. But we didn't move from the car and got through without being noticed. Along the road I glimpsed Cambodian flags every now and then, and each time I did so I gave a start, because they looked like North Korean flags . . . I thought it was the entrance to the North Korean embassy! My hand was tight around this car's door handle too.

Finally we arrived in the suburbs of Phnom Penh, in front of a building with very high walls and an automatic gate. I was more anxious than ever, telling myself that if this place was a trap there was no escape. I was already imagining the nightmare of the return to North Korea as a dire conclusion to our dangerous journey . . .

Inside, we found a large garden and a vast edifice. Imagine our surprise when we discovered that it provided shelter to about fifty North Koreans who had fled their country just as we had! They gave us a warm and open welcome. 'You're safe, don't worry, it's all going to be fine from now on!'

We then understood, with a great sigh of relief, that we could finally relax and sleep soundly. We were in good hands, the other North Koreans told us, pointing to the two strangers in dark glasses who had helped us and brought us to this unlikely refuge thousands of kilometres from the country we had fled. The first of these men was, it turned out, an employee of the South Korean embassy, the other a Protestant pastor.

Until then I knew absolutely nothing about religion. On arrival I got an edifying foretaste of it: a big cross stood in the hall of the building which was going to be our place of asylum until the next leg of our journey to South Korea. The day after our arrival, we were woken before dawn.

The pastor crossed the dormitories, calling, 'Hallelujah, hallelujah, it's time for prayer!' I looked through the window: it was still pitch dark outside! Numb with sleep, and still barely awake, we all followed our hosts into a large room where we were given bibles. After that we were made to sing hymns and say prayers before breakfast. Some refugees burst into tears during the service, contemplating the images of Jesus which they clutched between their hands and waved around. I couldn't understand what was happening, and I didn't know where I was.

The ritual also took place before every meal. It reminded me, strangely, of the ceremonies and political studies sessions to the glory of Kim Il-Sung and Kim Jong-Il, so I felt uneasy. But I should also say that I had never in my life seen such fervour, such emotion, such respect for others.

'President Song'

When the service had finished, I approached the pastor and asked him to help me bring my parents over from Manchuria. 'Fine, but we'll have to hurry,' he said, 'because the road between China and Indochina is starting to become too exposed, and will soon have to be abandoned in favour of another route.'

This was in 2001. The pastor sent two trusted colleagues to find my parents. A month and a half later, they passed through the gate of this great building just as I had done with Jin and Moon.

While waiting, I fell into line with the customs and routines of this strange community in which I was being held. We were forbidden to leave the property, for no one outside was to know of the existence of this providential refuge. To pass the time, I copied sacred images of Jesus. I also made a portrait of the pastor, who greatly appreciated it. I thought often about my mother and father, hoping that everything would go well, and dreaming of the new life that we would have in South Korea. The pastor told me to pray for God to protect them, so I did. Until the day they passed through the gate. What joy! What a relief!

My mother and father told me of their journey. They had followed the same route as we had, escorted by an experienced South Korean pastor who liked to be called 'President Song'. This was the man that 'my' pastor had entrusted with the mission of bringing back my parents. They were accompanied by an ethnically Korean Chinese man who acted as an assistant to 'President Song', and another would-be refugee. In the Chinese province of Jilin, the two smugglers picked up some more refugees, an old man and his wife. Once they reached Nanning, they all checked into a little hotel, using false identities. At four o'clock in the morning, the two smugglers set off to check the route. The road was clear, and all seven of them crossed the Vietnamese border. After a few hours' dangerous walk through jungle-covered mountains, and after taking a short rest, they took the train bound for Ho Chi Minh City. It takes three whole days to cross Vietnam, and once they were there the smugglers put them on a bus heading for the Cambodian border. The bus was followed by two motor-cyclists who were in league with the smugglers. At a bus stop, the smugglers made them get out. They were close to the border. Crammed on to the motorcycle seats, they drove for a few hours to a lake where boats waited to ferry them to the opposite shore. A few hours more on foot and they reached the border, which they crossed after 'President Song' had set off ahead as a scout. At last they were in Cambodia! In Phnom Penh, my father effusively thanked President Song. By now he had learned that in South Korea Song ran a company, of which he was the 'presi-dent', or director. 'I'd like to see you again in Seoul some day,' said my father. 'I'm sorry, but that won't be possible,' the 'President' replied. He had to protect his anonymity if he was to go on saving refugees.

Once our family had been reunited in Cambodia, we didn't stay very long in the pastor's big house. I had learned, in the meantime, that the organisation was financed by gifts from the Protestant community of South Korea. We travelled from Phnom Penh to Bangkok by plane, accompanied by another Protestant pastor who seemed to be in league with the embassy. We passed through customs with false passports, but got on to the Bangkok–Seoul plane without papers: South Korean diplomats walked us to the flight, through all the checkpoints. Upon our arrival, we were welcomed by agents of the *Angibu*.

9

Korean From Nowhere

Hanawon

Like all refugees coming to South Korea,* once we had arrived in Seoul we were sent to a special centre for adaptation to life in a capitalist society. This is a large modern building in the Seoul suburbs, called Hanawon. For two months, we took classes in which we were taught the ABC of everyday life: money, the underground, lodgings, the highway code, banks, how to find a job, payslips, law, justice, taxes, Social Security, electricity bills, and so on. We also had history classes, in which we had to seriously revise

---

* According to official South Korean figures, some three thousand North Koreans have managed to flee to South Korea, where they have settled. In fact the number is closer to ten thousand.

the notions inculcated in us in the North. We learned that Kim Il-Sung had spent many years in the Soviet Union, where his son Kim Jong-Il had been born – not in Korea as we had thought. But the most shocking thing for us was to learn that the Korean War had been started by Kim Il-Sung. In North Korea everyone believed that South Korea had attacked first! Our 'teachers' in Hanawon took us to the War Museum in Seoul to convince us otherwise. But even after this my father and I still had some doubts. It was only when talking to some South Koreans who put forward the same facts that we accepted that what we had just learned was true. Similarly, I had been unaware until coming to South Korea that the United States had dropped two atomic bombs on Japan. Neither did I know that it was the explosions in Hiroshima and Nagasaki that had driven the Japanese to surrender in 1945, and they had thus been obliged to withdraw from Korea, which they had occupied since 1910. In Onsong, we had been taught that it was Kim Il-Sung's armies that had defeated the Japanese, to drive them off our territory!

In fact, from the time I arrived in China I had begun to realise the extent to which we had been deluged with fairy-tales. The mere fact of discovering a prosperous China, where no one was dying of hunger, where all kinds of trade were possible, had come as a shock to me. So the world could be different! So hunger and indoctrination weren't inevitable! But the most emotional thing for me had been to see news footage of South Korea – a country that was universally condemned by the North, and that had always been presented to us as a kind of hell on earth. Yet these films depicted a South Korean reality that completely contradicted that demonised image. I will always remember the North Korean refugees in China passing these videos back and forth to one another in disbelief. Everyone, like me, ended up feeling hugely angry, terribly humiliated by the idea of having lived a sham, by the idea that most of the things we had learned in the North were not only useless, but they actually obstructed our thoughts. Nothing could be more degrading than to discover that you had been deceived by such a total lie, encompassing the whole of your existence. It forced you to question absolutely everything. Once I was in South Korea, that whole experience filled me with a spirit of rebellion that turned into hatred for Kim Jong-Il. If only I could wring his neck!

As I began to settle into my new life in Seoul, I had a recurring nightmare. I saw myself in China, and the Chinese police were taking me away, throwing me into prison and bringing me back to North Korea in chains. For months, this anxious dream haunted my nights. I woke up in a sweat very early in the morning and couldn't get back to sleep. I also often dreamed that I was returning illegally to North Korea to see my late grandfather. I have two friends in Seoul who are North Korean refugees like me. They too have had that obsessed nightmare of arrest in China and deportation to North Korea. They have other dreams as well, which we tell to each other because they remind us of North Korea. It's curious, but we do have a kind of nostalgia for hell. One of my friends once dreamed that he returned to the land of the two Kims with a machine-gun and killed everyone, as in a video game . . .

In South Korea, people are much more polite, more cultured and more honest than they are in the North. In the North you can't trust anyone. Swindlers roam the streets, and the need to survive, the greed provoked by hunger, can lead people to trick their fellow men, to steal from them, to fleece them unscrupulously of all they have. Lies, in North Korea, are indispensable for survival, and you have to be constantly on your guard. That is probably why, in South Korea, the people from the North are all considered to be potential criminals, liars, cheats and untrustworthy idlers. And that's hard for the refugees to live with.

Dwarves

I have now practically lost my Northern accent, which is a good thing, because of the anti-Northern discrimination.

Refugees are almost automatically excluded from proper employment. All they are left with is unqualified, temporary work. Certainly, they emerge from Hanawon armed with optimism and good resolutions, convinced that South Korea is a land of opportunities and welcome. But they very soon land with a bump. People are so suspicious of us that our hopes of a new life quickly evaporate. Many people end up completely demotivated. I know some who have slipped into alcoholism after going through the allowance of thirty million South Korean wons that the government gives each refugee to adapt to life in this country.

At the State school I go to, they call us 'dwarves' because we're so short. It is true that as a rule North Koreans are smaller than people from the South because, I would say, of the diet we were reduced to eating. In the face of such mockery, we Northerners generally react with violence. And when we hit, we hit hard, which doesn't go down well here. We risk going to prison. That's why it's better to keep your head down when people provoke you. But that's a difficult discipline for us to learn because it's through the use of force that we've managed to survive in the first place!

One of my two North Korean friends here has been unable to shed his accent. Whenever he takes a taxi, the driver asks him where he comes from. He says he's from the southern part of South Korea, another place where you could cut the accent with a knife. I've learned that it's essential to hide your origins, because when you tell people from here that you come from North Korea, though they're very sympathetic at first, it's not long before they won't think twice about humiliating you. To use a phrase from the North, 'they climb on your head to do their business on it'. The South Korean friends I used to see at the beginning asked me again and again to tell them about the famine in the North. I wanted to be friends with them, so I told them, again and again. But in the end I became the class whipping-boy. Like all North Koreans who have been through what I've been through, I'm very easily riled. We have been utterly humiliated, so the slightest dodgy remark makes our hair stand on end. The survival reflexes that we've learned in the North are hard to shake off. I've known some refugees who've left their houses, fought with their colleagues, can't bear any kind of discipline and sometimes even take their own lives.

A serious incident happened in a Seoul secondary school in March 2003. Two Northerners who had endured whole days of teasing called on all the other Northerners they knew for help. I was one of them. About twenty of us, all from different schools, went on a punitive expedition. We turned up at the school in broad daylight, armed with billiard balls and who knows what else. There was a monumental ruckus. We sent tons of the Southern bullies to hospital. The others got the fright of their life. The teachers who tried to calm us down took a few good thumps as well. So much so that the police finally intervened. After that, the parents of the Southerners claimed financial compensation of ten million South Korean wons. The claims were subject to lengthy negotiations, but fortunately the teachers managed to sort things out. The rules are very different here; if there's a fight in the North, the one who provoked it is the one who takes the rap, whereas here, even if you're provoked, it's better not to respond, because the one who deals the first blow is the one who gets punished. In the North the cause is what's important, while in the South it's the result that matters. I think it's more unjust in the South.

This episode had another unfortunate consequence: it alerted people in my school to the fact that I was originally from North Korea. My main concern up until then, like that of my Northern schoolmates, lay in hiding my origins in order to avoid being a target for mockery. When people got suspicious about us because of our accents, we explained that we had lived in China, or that we were Southerners from Pusan, or that we were rural, backward yokels. But it was hard to explain away our small physique, which became a major handicap to our assimilation. The most unbearable thing was to hear kids two or three years younger than us, who knew absolutely nothing about life, telling us right in the middle of the classroom to go and 'play with the little ones'. It always ended in a punch-up. Our limited vocabulary gave us away as well. The fact that we didn't know fashionable words, most of them derived from English, exposed us to everyone's scorn. Despite this, in South Korea the most exciting thing for me is the sense of feeling free. It's an emotion that fills my whole body. In North Korea, we were brought up not to aspire to freedom.

But how can I not feel humiliated in this modern country of plenty, which may have taken us in but looks down on us as inferiors? Whatever I might have lived through before, whatever the dangers may have been, the blindness, the forced stupidity, the constant terror, the hunger, the sickness, the persecutions, those bits of life are a part of me and will always be etched within me. I may have fled them, but I can't deny them. It seems to be a common paradox among refugees, this joy at being in a free country, mixed with nostalgia for the nightmare landscapes that we have fled.

After the incident in March 2003, most schools in Seoul refused to accept North Korean students, regarding them as thugs. So we are now forced to go to specialist private institutions. The government, which is very concerned about this phenomenon of rejection, is trying to set up a remedial course for refugees: junior and secondary school education covered in four years of study.

Four years! That's too long for me. I want to study art, but how can I wait another four years? My mother is asking me to take these remedial classes, but it's very hard for me to concentrate on theoretical classes when I'm used to living independently, sorting things out for myself and being self-sufficient. I've sometimes skipped school for several weeks with other friends from the North, to earn a little money, and we've been taken on as temporary workers on a building site for a stadium, installing artificial turf, transporting iron rods . . .

The Northerners all tend to fall back on one another's company rather than trying to adapt, and end up spending most evenings together. We have a fantastic time. But at parties where Southerners are present, we're superfluous. We can't even joke with them. Our sense of humour is very different; the people from the South don't laugh at our jokes, and vice versa.

It's hard for me to leave my Northern friends, with whom I have become very close, because of our shared experiences. Sometimes each of us has important things to be getting on with; but we can't leave one another! So we stay together. They remind me of Choljin, Kuanyok and Kuanjin, my dear friends that I abandoned in North Korea. All four of us, I remember, had the same dream: to become painters or draftsmen. That ideal kept us together, perhaps because drawing was our way of transfiguring our world.

That's probably why I go on drawing. Everywhere, all the time. As though it is only when recreated by the tip of my pencil that life assumes its full weight, its full significance: that of reality.

Do Choljin, Kuanyok and Kuanjin still draw? Do they think of me the way I think of them? I'm sure I'll see those dear friends again one day . . . after the reunification of Korea, in ten years, perhaps, or a bit more.

And what a party we'll throw when we finally meet again!

Appendix

Penal Labour Colonies
in North Korea

(Source: *US Committee for human rights in North Korea*,
report published in October 2003.)

There are three kinds of gulag:

Kwanli-so, literally 'control camp', which can be translated as 'political penal labour colony'. North Korea officially denies their existence. They are run under the auspices of the *Kukga Bowibu* (Department of National Security). Between one hundred and fifty and two hundred thousand people are subjected to forced labour in them. A person sentenced for a political crime is locked up with his whole family or part of it, according to the principle in force in North Korea of 'collective responsibility' and *yeon jwa je* (guilt by association). Along with the prisoners themselves, three generations, brothers and sisters, father and mother, children and sometimes grandchildren, are currently incarcerated (in 1972, the Great Leader had said that 'Factionalists or enemies of class must be eliminated through three generations').

The number of family members thrown into the camp depends on the gravity of the 'crime'. None of the prisoners is, officially speaking, 'judged'. There is no judicial process, and prisoners are incarcerated on the basis of 'confessions', often extracted under torture.

The prisoners, whether they be adults, old people or children, have practically no chance of getting out, and a sentence generally amounts to a whole life of slave labour in mines, cement factories, sawmills or very special prison-farms. One of the camps, however, camp number 15 in Yodok, has a 're-education' section from which one can be freed. That was what happened to the grandson of a political prisoner whose entire family had been thrown into the camp, Kang Cholhwan. He was imprisoned from 1977 until 1987, between the ages of nine and nineteen.* These *kwanli-so* are located in remote areas of the country, and sometimes cover a surface area of tens of square kilometres. Because of insufficient rations, bad treatment and the harshness of the forced labour, a considerable proportion of these prisoners die fairly quickly. But the contingent is constantly replaced.

---

* His testimony is published in *Aquariums of Pyongyang: Ten Years in the North Korean Gulag*, by Kang Chol-Hwan and Pierre Rigoulot, Basic Books, 2001.

Appendix

The *kyohwa-so*, literally 're-education camps', come under the control of the Department of Popular Security (*Inmin Boanseong*). They are sometimes large penitentiaries surrounded by walls, barbed wire and watch-towers, and sometimes enormous camps surrounded by barbed wire and located in remote valleys, where the prisoners are forced to work in the mines. As in the *kwanli-so*, work is extremely hard, food rations are inadequate and the mortality rate is so high that the prisoners call them 'death camps'. The difference from the *kwanli-so* is that political prisoners and prisoners of common law are mixed together, and that sentences have been pronounced after a judicial process. Whereas in the *kwanli-so* most prisoners are serving life sentences, the detainees in the *kyohwa-so* are serving fixed sentences. Some of them have been sentenced for private trade without permission, or for smuggling goods across the border with China.

Another system of very special camps exists along the Sino-Korean border. The North Korean authorities have called these local gulags *rodong danryeondae* (colonies for re-education through labour) and *jipkyul so* (collective colonies). Having first appeared after the famine broke out in the early nineties, these improvised gulags serve to punish North Koreans who have been repatriated after escaping to China, or who have been discovered in North

Korea after returning from China. But at a local level they are also used almost routinely to punish any breaches of strict social discipline provoked by the famine: absenteeism in the workplace, theft of food from the fields, private trade without permission or travelling outside the village without a permit.

Other outrages, such as humming a South Korean song, when they are not punished in the *kwanli-so*, can land the offender in a re-education through labour camp. The period of detention does not generally exceed six months in the 'collective camps', but it can be even shorter (a few months) in the 'camps of re-education by labour', which are scattered around the countryside, the towns and villages. The work there is hard, rations are tiny, and many people die before completing their sentences. To avoid burdening the administration of the camps with sick people or pointless deaths, prisoners who are about to die of hunger, exhaustion or various diseases are sent home on 'sick leave'. The convalescent's health is monitored by neighbours who are given the task of spying on him several times a day. As soon as he recovers, he is sent back to the labour colony.

Also published by Abacus

SURVIVING THE SWORD

Brian MacArthur

Many of the British, Australian and American prisoners held by the Japanese during the Second World War were so scarred by their experiences that afterwards they could not discuss them even with their families. They believed that their brutal treatment by Japanese and Korean guards was, literally, incomprehensible.

But some prisoners were determined that posterity should know how they were starved and beaten, marched almost to death or transported on 'hellships', and used as slave labour – most notoriously on the Burma-Thailand railway – and how thousands died from tropical diseases. They risked torture and execution to keep secret diaries and make sketches and drawings that they hid from the guards wherever they could, sometimes burying them in the graves of lost comrades.

The diaries tell of inhumanity and degradation, but there are also inspirational stories of courage, comradeship and compassion: how the men cared for the sick, risked death to steal from the Japanese; staged shows, concerts and cricket matches in the jungle; made secret radios; and how the doctors operated – and saved lives – with razors and butcher's saws.

Brian MacArthur has spent most of his career on *The Times*, where he was an executive editor. He was also deputy editor of the *Sunday Times*, founder editor of the *Times Higher Education Supplement* and Eddy Shah's *Today*. He lives in London and Norfolk.

ABACUS
978-0-349-11937-3

THEY WOULD NEVER HURT A FLY

Slavenka Drakulić

The breaking up of Yugoslavia in the 1990s brought with it a cruelty and brutality that few thought Europe would ever see again. Acclaimed novelist and journalist Slavenka Drakulić reports from the War Crimes Tribunal in The Hauge, to try to learn from and understand these events.

As well as witnessing the trial of Slobodan Milošęvić she focuses on the lesser men, the ordinary individuals whose power did not extend beyond their village or their town borders. Men such as Goran Jelisić, a volunteer policeman, who executed many of his prisoners, or Dražen Erdemović, a participant in the massacre of seven thousand Muslims in Srebrenica. It is their ordinariness that makes their crimes so shocking: the fact that the crimes were carried out not by regular soldiers, but by former waiters, drivers and fishermen.

But for all the horrors, there is hope here too: that justice offers future generations the chance to escape the shadow of the past.

ABACUS
978-0-349-11775-1

ONE PALESTINE, COMPLETE

Tom Segev

Tom Segev's widely acclaimed work has changed the way we view the history of Israel. Now, in this new book, he discusses the three decades when Palestine was ruled by the British Empire; and Britain's promise to both Jews and Arabs that they would inherit the land.

Segev reconstructs in vivid detail the tumultuous era when anything seemed possible and everything went awry. Here are the legendary figures – General Allenby, Lawrence of Arabia, King Faisal, Chaim Weizmann and David Ben-Gurion, all participants in a multicultural spectacle of revolution and decadence, prophecy and illusion.

One Palestine, Complete is a stunning history of a dramatic period that witnessed the decline of an empire, the birth of one nation and the tragedy of another.

'A full and fascinating account of the murky roots of British rule in Palestine. [Segev's] treatment of the Balfour Declaration is a good example of the originality, insight and rigorous objectivity that shine through the entire book . . . Segev makes an immensely valuable contribution to the existing literature both with the new information he has unearthed and by suggesting fresh interpretations . . . wide-ranging and elegantly written' *Literary Review*

'Brilliantly written . . . wonderfully readable and humane' *Independent*

'A magisterial account . . . reaffirms Segev's reputation for courageous and intelligent honesty' *Scotsman*

ABACUS
978-0-349-11286-2

A MORAL RECKONING

Daniel Jonah Goldhagen

'A compelling, challenging and important book that, God willing, will not become yet another indictment that the Vatican simply sweeps under the carpet' *Independent on Sunday*

From the internationally renowned author of the bestselling *Hitler's Willing Executioners*, *A Moral Reckoning* is a penetrating moral inquiry into the Catholic Church's role in the Holocaust that goes beyond anything previously written on the subject.

Daniel Jonah Goldhagen shows that the Church has, even according to its own doctrine, an unacknowledged duty of repair. He explores it, analyses the Church's tactics of evasion, and delineates all that the Church must do to repair the harm it inflicted on Jews, and to heal itself.

Brilliantly researched and reasoned, *A Moral Reckoning* is a path-breaking book of profound, and potentially explosive, importance.

'[*A Moral Reckoning*] breaks important new ground . . . Not a word is wasted in a book that can only be read with profit by all' *Spectator*

ABACUS
978-0-349-11693-8

Now you can order superb titles directly from Abacus

☐ Surviving the Sword	Brian MacArthur	£9.99
☐ They Would Never Hurt a Fly	Slavenka Drakulić	£9.99
☐ One Palestine, Complete	Tom Segev	£14.99
☐ A Moral Reckoning	Daniel Jonah Goldhagen	£9.99

The prices shown above are correct at time of going to press. However, the publishers reserve the right to increase prices on covers from those previously advertised, without further notice.

──────────────── ⬭ ABACUS ⬭ ────────────────

Please allow for postage and packing: **Free UK delivery.**
Europe; add 25% of retail price; Rest of World; 45% of retail price.

To order any of the above or any other Abacus titles, please call our credit card orderline or fill in this coupon and send/fax it to:

Abacus, P.O. Box 121, Kettering, Northants NN14 4ZQ
Fax: 01832 733076   Tel: 01832 737526
Email: aspenhouse@FSBDial.co.uk

☐ I enclose a UK bank cheque made payable to Abacus for £ . . . .
☐ Please charge £ . . . . . . to my Visa, Delta, Maestro.

Expiry Date ⬚⬚⬚⬚   Maestro Issue No. ⬚⬚

NAME (BLOCK LETTERS please) . . . .

ADDRESS . . . .

. . . .

. . . .

Postcode . . . . Telephone . . . .

Signature . . . .

Please allow 28 days for delivery within the UK. Offer subject to price and availability.